MY NAME IS

Javeria K. Shah

MY NAME IS

Is Your Name a Gift or a Burden?

The Cultural Anthropology Collection

Collection Editors

Nila Ginger Hofman & Janise Hurtig

LPp

First published in 2024 by Lived Places Publishing

British Library Cataloguing in Publication Data
A CIP record for this book is available from the British Library

ISBN: 9781915734235 (pbk)
ISBN: 9781915734259 (ePDF)
ISBN: 9781915734242 (ePUB)

Cover design by Fiachra McCarthy
Book design by Rachel Trolove of Twin Trail Design
Typeset by Newgen Publishing UK

Lived Places Publishing
Long Island
New York 11789

www.livedplacespublishing.com

Acknowledgements

I am grateful to my parents for giving me a beautiful name and for helping me stay connected to my heritage. I am happy that I have found my way back to Javeria, and as a result, have found myself. I would like to express my deepest gratitude to Tony Giroux for recognising the depth and story behind a small teaching moment. I will always be thankful to you for bringing this project to life in your beautiful film. A special thanks to Pereko Makgothi and Kristina Lao for their incredible support for this project and for being a part of the My Name Is team; you are amazing! This book acknowledges and thanks all the wonderful participants who have shared their stories with us. It is dedicated to all those outstanding individuals who encounter challenges and barriers in navigating their name identity daily. I hear you, see you, and stand with you in solidarity.

I would like to express my sincere appreciation to all my colleagues at the Royal Central School of Speech and Drama, University of London, for quickly adapting to my reverting to my given name. I appreciate you all so much. Special thanks to Kate McCurdy for swiftly making changes across all outward-facing platforms and keeping me involved at all points, to Megan Hunter for supporting my name transition across Central, and last but never least, Josette Bushell-Mingo for your continuous support for this project and for recognising its value.

I want to express my sincere gratitude to everyone who shared their stories for this book. I apologise that not all accounts were included, but please be assured that your stories are still a great source of inspiration for this project. I hope to utilise your powerful experiences in future projects.

I want to thank everyone who has taken extra care to learn and correctly pronounce a name. You make more of a positive impact than you may realise. For all of you who have reached out to us to let us know how this project has positively impacted you or led you to deep reflection, we have been so moved by your feedback and appreciate your support of the project. Please keep spreading the word because names matter!

Abstract

This book explores the difficulties faced by individuals with non-Western names living in the West. It originated from a research project that began as a university lecture I was leading. It elaborates on how a teaching moment led to a collaboration with one of my students, Tony Giroux, to create an accompanying multi-award-winning short documentary series called *My Name Is*.

The book delves deeper into the issues discussed in the documentary and provides additional accounts of individuals who have faced challenges related to their name identity in various situations. I also introduce my original Whiteness ecology theory to explain how colonialism and systemic barriers have impacted people's sense of social belonging.

My objective is to start an honest and open conversation about name identity and to promote inclusivity through this book.

Keywords

Name bias
Anglicising names
Names in education
Names in society
Western norms
Name identity

Contents

Introduction

My Name Is is a project inspired by a screen studies class I facilitated at the Royal Central School of Speech and Drama, University of London. While facilitating icebreakers with the cohort of primarily international students, I took extra care in correctly pronouncing individual names. Filmmaker and actor Tony Giroux, a student in the class, asked why I was taking such care in getting people's names right. He was curious why this mattered so much to me. The question was simple, but in answering it, I began a long journey of introspection that would surpass the classroom and seep into all aspects of my life. In my response to Tony, I risked trust and vulnerability before the class, disclosing that I wasn't born as "Jo" (an anglicised name I had used for over 20+ years) and that my given name was Javeria. I had changed it to assimilate, to avoid attention being drawn to me, to make others struggling with its pronunciation feel more comfortable, and above all, to avoid name bias associated with navigating a non-western name in Western contexts.

Tony continued pondering my disclosure and this classroom interaction for some time, and months later, he approached me again. He asked me more questions and expressed an interest in articulating a film that would capture my story and those of others around names. Until this point, I had never realised the significance of my experience in its resonance with others. I suggested a social awareness-raising research project that a film could be one articulation of, and we successfully applied for funding, which formed the first stage of the My Name Is research project.

Tony and I began this project with a teacher student relationship background that evolved into a collaborative dynamic as a result of this project. Our research dynamic was unique relative to traditional research approaches. As we found out, it was also the strength of our project. By consciously aiming to dismantle power dynamics, we could work together to create spaces for stories and personal truths. Our participants risked trust and vulnerability to authentically share their experiences because of the relationships forged with the project team over time. Accounts shared in the film included references to name bias and, subsequently, pressure to anglicise names to overcome systemic barriers to success, as well as recollections of navigating hostile spaces and associated negative experiences relating to non-Western names in Western contexts. Film participant accounts are shared in this book's early chapters for a more in-depth insight into the authentic and vulnerable narratives shared.

Before embarking on this project, I was "Jo", but in 2020, a year after the film's release, I chose to revert to my given name, Javeria. This project changed my life. It brought me back to my given name and helped me reclaim my lost identity. After sharing my story for the film, I began reflecting deeply on why I had changed my name and considering what a return to my given name might look like in practical terms. It was a decision I agonised over for more than a year until I finally gathered the courage to reclaim my original name. In 2020, I announced the change on Twitter (now X) and began communicating it across all my professional and social networks. The support I received in reclaiming my name was incredible from colleagues and friends, and my networks, in general, motivated me to continue with confidence.

Since its release, this project and associated film have reached thousands of people with a message of hope, listening to understand, respect, and empathy surrounding names and a sense of social belonging. Every film screening we have hosted has led to profoundly poignant and powerful disclosures from our audiences. Many of our film audience members have approached us with their own stories and, through doing so, signify the importance of names. We have heard from the Jewish diaspora disclosing the changing of surnames in their recent ancestry for safety, trans communities discussing the significance of the names that are chosen to represent identity, and the Irish diaspora have shared the significance of religious identity through names and historically what this has meant in connection to safety. The themes of this project have resonated with so many, and feedback from our audiences has been a crucial motivator for us to continue spreading messages of inclusion and respect.

I was particularly moved by the support we received from the Swansea-based organisation Ways of Working, who disseminated our call-out for more participants for the book phase with the *Street Matters* community. Community stories reflected the overarching themes to have emerged in the film and now in this book in the shape of:

- Encountering racism because of name bias;
- Bullying at school due to having an unusual name;
- Shortening or changing names for the comfort and ease of others;
- Name mispronunciation;
- Name bias.

Building on the focus of the *My Name Is* film, this book recognises the significance of lived experiences to understand the impact of name navigations on personal identity formation. Grounded in new accounts while acknowledging the stories shared in the associated film, this book extends focus into the counter-narratives relating to navigating name identities in the authentic voices of participants – and continues the conversation around names and their importance to our identity formation and sense of individual social belonging.

I begin by sharing an original theoretical framework that I developed in 2021. This framework, called "Whiteness ecology", offers readers tools to understand marginalised groups' experiences from a broader contextual perspective. I introduce this theory and summarise how it can be applied to five stories featured in the associated *My Name Is* film. These stories comprise the book's first five chapters, and serve as an example of the theory's application in name-navigation contexts. Readers are then invited to explore the other stories in this book by applying the Whiteness ecology theory, should they wish to delve deeper into the stories. In the process, some readers develop an empathetic and holistic understanding of the challenges marginalised communities face in navigating their identities. These new stories are also laid out differently from the first five chapters, as the new participants share their contexts in their own words.

1
Understanding name identity using Whiteness ecology theory

- The reader will become familiarised with the author's Whiteness ecology theory and be able to apply this to the name stories shared in this book.
- The reader will be able to develop an understanding of the deeper issues relating to navigating names in Western contexts through applying this theory.
- The reader will be able to use this theory in other contexts where applicable.

Classifications

Throughout this chapter and book, I will be referencing non-white racialisations as melanin-rich or global majority to counteract terms such as BAME (Black, Asian, Minority, Ethnic). This is in line with my anti-racist activism and its emphasis on the significance of language as a tool to classify individuals racialised as "Non-White". Existing terms such as "Black" or "Brown" will only be used in their original citation contexts or connection to specific discourse or data references.

What is Whiteness ecology?

Whiteness ecology (Shah, 2021) combines two distinct theoretical positions. The first is inspired by Bronfenbrenner's (1975) bio-ecological theory, which presents society using an ecology metaphor. The second derives from the work of critical Whiteness theorist Nayak (2007), who contends that:

1. Whiteness is a modern invention; it has changed over time and place;
2. Whiteness is a social norm and has become chained to an index of unspoken privileges;
3. The bonds of Whiteness can yet be broken/deconstructed for the betterment of humanity.

(2007, p. 738)

Whiteness ecology aligns with the "third wave" (Garner, 2017, p. 1583) of critical Whiteness, which aims to extend the focus on Whiteness in the context of power dynamics (Shah, 2021, p. 280). This chapter will explain Whiteness ecology theory and its filtering down of Whiteness across social systems.

This chapter now shifts to a more detailed consideration of Bronfenbrenner's bio-ecological theory in connection to Whiteness so that the accounts shared in the associated *My Name Is* film can be more carefully considered.

Ecological Whiteness

Whiteness ecology is premised on the theorisation that Whiteness is ideological and upheld through white supremacy and its associated social classifications represent ideological (Western) colonial legacies that othered indigenous groups and cultures, and organised human worth based on race, with Whiteness being at the top of the so-called hierarchy. Whiteness ecology considers how stratifying ideological legacies filter down across social structures, systems, and interactions within the Global North and post-/still colonial spaces (Shah, 2021). The overarching premise of the bio-ecological theory is "… modelled using interconnecting layers constituting of a chronosystem, macrosystem, exosystem, mesosystem, and microsystem" (2021, p. 281).

Figure 1 illustrates the interconnected and cyclical nature of various systems. The diagram includes both inner and outer layers, which are linked to each other. At the centre of the diagram, we have the individual and their social characteristics such as age, gender, and race. This is where we can begin to understand whether the individual has any traits that could differentiate them from their broader environment. We can then analyse the macro and micro impacts of these traits on the individual which can be understood using the analogy of a ripple effect (Hong and Garbarino, 2012, p. 276). When considering Whiteness and British Muslim individuals, understanding each layer helps to visualise the broader context.

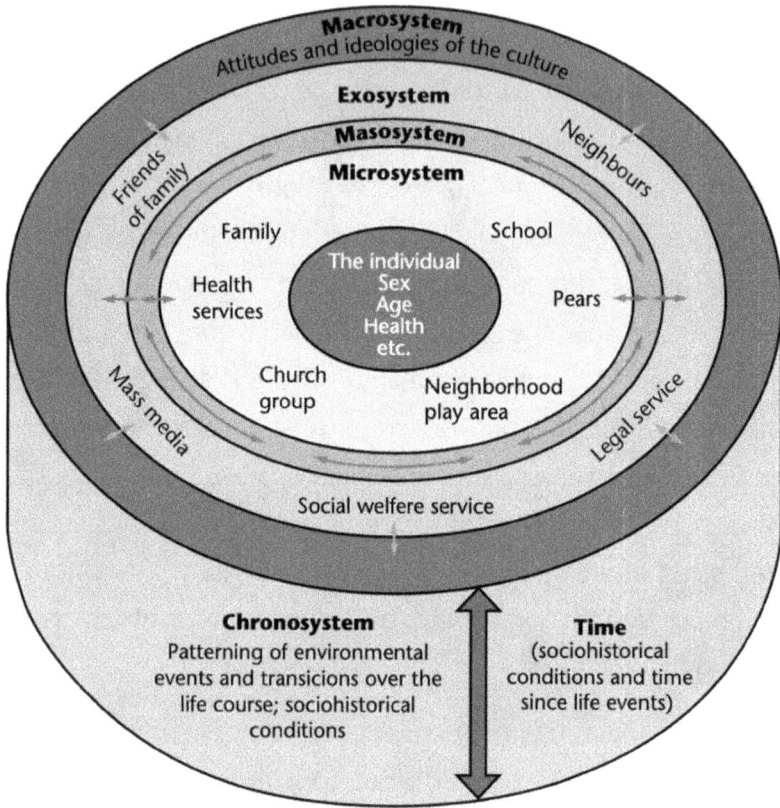

Figure 1 Bio-Ecological Theory. Source: Santrock (2007). *Child Development,* 11th ed. NY: McGraw-Hill Companies Inc.

Chronosystem

The ecology is surrounded by the chronosystem, which represents the social and historical contexts over time for the individual. This backdrop may include post-9/11 policy impacts that affect Muslim communities disproportionately, such as the Prevent Duty in the UK that has had a negative impact on Muslim communities. As a result, under the Prevent Duty, Muslims are statistically more likely to be subjected to negative classifications that will negatively impact their life trajectories in shape of educational and professional opportunities.

Macrosystem and exosystem

The system that perpetuates Whiteness often leads to the formation of dominant social beliefs that stereotype marginalised racial communities negatively, both on a larger social level and in external systems. This is further reinforced by the depictions and coverage of mainstream media, which exists outside of the immediate system. The external system also represents the spread of dominant beliefs, attitudes, and cultures to the individual through social constructs such as family, friends, and legal and welfare systems.

A visibly Muslim individual who is positioned at the centre of this exosystem is likely to experience racial microaggressions based on negative ideological assumptions that categorise Muslims as a social threat or violent terrorists. This broader system dynamic can affect their experiences in various ways. For instance, news coverage in the UK and US often equates terrorism with Muslims and shows racial bias in the reporting of terror attacks.

In practical terms, being visibly Muslim can lead to varying degrees of insecurity across all levels of society. For example, after a terrorist attack for which a Muslim person may be held responsible, Muslims may become extremely cautious about how they are perceived by their neighbours and friends. They may also worry about the impact of this on the larger community through moral panics, which can lead to increased referrals under the Prevent Duty. This, in turn, can affect the quality of their interactions with social welfare and legal systems.

Mesosystem and microsystem

The mesosystem refers to the interaction between larger social structures (exosystem) and the immediate environment (microsystem). This provides access to social systems on a small scale. To illustrate, let's consider the scenario of a Muslim individual and the Prevent Duty. In this context, we can observe the mesosystem in the school environment. For instance, if a teacher makes a Prevent referral, it can potentially have negative consequences for the life and prospects of a young Muslim who is subjectively perceived as a potential threat.

These layers form part of a holistic ecosystem that enables better insights into an individual's social navigation and associated experiences. Subsequently, this leads to multiple social interaction possibilities while acknowledging that the experiences of melanin-rich or global majority individuals, or those from historically or presently colonised diasporas, are more likely to be marginalised in Whiteness ecology that positions Whiteness as a normative (Shah, 2021).

In practical terms, this theory can be applied to various Western social contexts. For instance, several research studies have confirmed that Black boys are marginalised within the UK education system through disproportionately punitive measures such as school detentions, suspension, or expulsion. Furthermore, several studies have also revealed a pattern in such measures negatively impacting Black boys' future journeys, resulting in academic failure, incarceration, or severe mental health classifications. These research findings are represented in disproportionate Black male representation within the UK criminal and mental health systems.

Importantly, research also reveals that young white males in the UK from similar social backgrounds in terms of class and academic ability have comparatively positive educational and social experiences. Understanding this phenomenon through the lens of Whiteness ecology, we can see the following factors come into play:

- Based on Western colonial constructions of a hierarchy of race and those racialised as non-white are at the bottom. Black boys are negatively classified in line with colonial ideological legacies.
- Negative classifications include their adultification (treating children as adults and holding them accountable in such ways), criminalising them, and labelling them as "stupid" or aggressive and mentally ill.
- Such classifications create a social barrier for Black boys and men.
- These barriers can be understood by observing social structures, systems, and interactions. For example, in addition to the example cited above, Black boys and men in the UK are most likely to be stopped and searched by the police.
- This example represents the filtering down of racialised colonial ideologies that cause harm to Black boys and men in the UK in all areas of their social lives.

It is, however, worth noting that in developing a Whiteness ecology, I do recognise the nuances within Whiteness itself and the complexities of navigating this identity in the context of marginalised ethnicities such as Jewish, Irish, or Gypsy Roma/Irish Traveller communities. Furthermore, I also acknowledge that a low socio-economic background or other marginalisations would also impact full access to white privilege, as this is heavily tied into hetero normative, elite, heterosexual male privilege (Etchells *et al.*, 2017). However, despite access to full privilege, the experiences of someone racialised as white in comparison to someone who is black or brown who isn't located within the Whiteness ecology will be vastly different because of the colonial racial binaries of white in opposition to black and brown.

Looking more carefully at Bronfenbrenner's (1975) ecology layers in Figure 1 below, we can see the interconnectivity between each layer across contexts and time and its extension from ideological to social interaction.

To frame Bronfenbrenner's (1975) model as a Whiteness ecology, I treat each component through the lens of Euro-colonialism, associated white supremacy, and the subsequent experiences of global majorities navigating this ecology. The following section expands on this using the UK context and then shifts to applying this theory to identity contexts and name navigation to frame the subsequent chapters.

I start with the outward chronosystem layer, representing time and socio-historical conditions. In a Whiteness ecology, this would be represented in the accumulation of negative experiences over time for the melanated/global majority individual. These experiences would take shape in racial microaggressions and/or systemic or structural racism, represented by a lack of access to education or opportunities. This could also be linked to global majority community contexts. For example, in the UK context, the Black British[1] experience could be connected to a range of socio-historic contexts such as British colonialism of the West

Indies, Windrush migration, contemporary histories of strained relations between Black communities and the police (Shah, 2021), and racism such as in a British education system that negatively classified young Black learners as *subnormal* throughout the 1960s and 1970s (*Subnormal*, 2021).

Shifting from these examples into the macrosystem layer, which represents cultural ideologies and attitudes, in a Whiteness ecology, dominant social and political ideologies uphold white supremacy. Dominant colonial ideologies are represented in the exosystem layer in our interactions and engagements with our wider social circles, neighbours, state services, or the mainstream media we consume, which generates and reinforces negative racial stereotypes such as Muslims as terrorists, Black women as angry, or Black men as criminal, and perpetuates social intolerance for groups. An example of such programming includes BBC sitcoms such as *Dad's Army* or British films such as *Carry On Up the Khyber*, which use brown faces and exaggerated Indian accents to represent South Asian communities. Legacy colonial ideologies that continue to hegemonically reenforce racial, linguistic, cultural, and ethnic othering are representative of socially constructed racial hierarchies that position Whiteness as the default and the normative as invisible, free of critique or scrutiny.

We can see this play out in the quality of representations in the mainstream media (Hall, 1997), the state's micromanaged curriculum through educational policy churn (Steer *et al.*, 2007) and associated omissions of our colonial past from the curriculum, and in the introduction of policymaking, such as the Prevent

Duty, or through policy levered legal systems that disproportionately target racially marginalised groups such as the stop and
search laws in the UK (Shah, 2021). The Prevent Duty is a post-9/
11 policy lever which awards all UK public sector organisations
such as schools, social services, and the national health services
the capacity to classify individuals as at risk of radicalisation
based on their racial embodiments and Muslimness. The policy
has disproportionately and unfairly caused negative and unfair
repercussions for many Muslims in the UK. A recent High Court
ruling concluded that parts of the policy wording were racist and
should be redrafted. This hegemonic dynamic can also be seen
to play out in the mesosystem of a Whiteness ecology.

The final parts of this ecology metaphor constitute the individual
at the very centre and their microsystem layer. In a Whiteness
ecology, the individual's racial, ethnic, or cultural background will
determine the quality of their social experiences and access to
opportunities.

Here's a clearer and error-free version of it:

When a person with a non-western name interacts in a predominantly white environment, they may face difficulties navigating their name. This issue is closely linked to the manifestation
of unconscious colonial biases. In the "My Name Is" film, several
individuals with non-western names faced this challenge. As
someone who has experienced this in the past, I can relate to
feeling like an outsider due to the mispronunciation of my name
by teachers. This experience negatively impacted my sense of
belonging.

By applying the concept of Whiteness ecology to name navigation, we can gain a more comprehensive understanding of the
social contexts and impacts involved. I am suggesting that it is
not merely a matter of mispronouncing someone's name and
causing them discomfort, but rather that there are broader impli-
cations to name navigation that pertain to issues such as coloni-
sation, racial politics, and hegemony.

2
My name is Javeria

Exploring race and name identity through the author's autoethnography

- Readers will interpret Javeria's story using Whiteness ecology to understand name navigation in the context of race.
- Educators and leaders will be motivated to prepare and implement inclusive, holistic, pedagogic, and professional practices regarding names, with an aim to facilitate cultures of racial belonging.

Introduction

This chapter marks a shift in writing style as I share mine and others' name stories in our own words. This is so that you, as the reader, can connect with us and understand our experiences and perspectives. All accounts, including mine, are drawn verbatim from the associated *My Name Is* film.

This and each subsequent chapter will allow you to consider our stories through a Whiteness ecology lens to understand wider social contexts, but essentially, we invite you to engage with our stories so that you can begin seeing the people behind the stories and appreciate the importance of name identity to individual experience.

Meet "Jo", the artist formerly known as "Javeria"

My name is Jo. I was born Javeria, and that was my given name. I became conscious at quite an early age that the name was quite problematic to pronounce in a British context. When I became older, I came across other people who had complicated names and had changed them to anglicised ones. I noticed there was a currency to having an anglicised name. It was easier to pronounce, you were accepted a bit more, and you didn't have to go through that embarrassment of being made to feel different. So, I changed to Jo informally when I was around 13–14 and then officially started going by that name in college from 16 onwards. I needed to almost reinvent myself and use that name with people that didn't know me. For any new acquaintanceship I made, I would use the name, Jo; that's how it phased in. It was instantaneous. I just felt more accepted. It got to the point where if my given name was ever used I felt like I was in trouble because I stopped identifying with it.

Jo came from Joey. I wasn't abbreviating my given name. My parents liked nicknames. We all (siblings) had nicknames. My nickname was Joey, which devastated me for a long time because it's either a baby kangaroo or a boy's name. But then, thankfully, or not, *Dawson's Creek* came onto the scene, and they had the female Joey character, which suddenly made it a little bit more acceptable – but by that time, I had become Jo already, so it was too late to revert back to Joey. Maybe if I'd gone to my nickname, I would have probably felt more secure because it was my name, Joey. But instead, I was drawn to the idea of something that was the opposite of my given name. It was short, it didn't have very many syllables, it was easy to spell, it was easy to say. I had gone for something extreme; I've gone from something really complicated to something extreme.

The periods I grew up in weren't very inclusion-literate, if that makes sense. So, you didn't really have concepts of inclusion and diversity. Some people argue there's a lot of lip service around these issues nowadays, and there probably is. Nevertheless, that conscious awareness to try and address those issues wasn't there as much when I was growing up. I think we've moved towards a more positive direction in that I don't think a lot of people would feel the need to have to adopt an Anglo name. Or at least I hope they wouldn't. However, this said, there are recent statistics that were shared with us in an unconscious bias training course which confirmed that people with foreign-sounding names are less likely to be shortlisted for jobs in the UK. I've certainly had that experience. I've applied as Javeria, and I've applied as Jo with the exact same CV for the exact same role. Sadly, Javeria wasn't shortlisted, but Jo made it through all application and interview rounds and was offered the role.

Struggling with "Javeria"

I studied in London and all my teachers from Primary school to college struggled in pronouncing my name.

It got to a point where I knew my name was about to come up on the register because of the way everything was alphabetised using surnames. I knew when my name was about to come and I could recognise the teachers struggling and pondering how he or she would say the name. (I remember) feeling really embarrassed as if attention was being drawn to me or was about to be drawn to me in an uncomfortable way because they used to always attempt to say my name in lots of different ways, none of which were quite right. I'd always just say, "Here!" quickly because I didn't want them to have to even try to pronounce the name. I used to find it really embarrassing.

The way teachers handled my name made me more conscious of it in a negative way. With my friends, they would usually say something like "That's a beautiful name" or "I like your name". If my friends were not familiar with my name, they would respectfully learn how to pronounce it properly. It wasn't really an issue with my friends probably because I grew up in a diverse part of London where everyone respected each other's cultures. However, with authority figures, I felt like they saw me as a complicated name on the register that would present a challenge in terms of having to say it out loud. This made me feel dehumanised.

As we're discovering through statistics, even the most diverse (geographical) areas have white systems and structures. For example, several ethnically diverse London boroughs do not represent their make-up in local public service senior leadership teams, such as education and health and social care services that serve the local areas.

I had some white inspirational teachers and authority figures who inspired me in many ways. Ethnicity and race didn't (explicitly) frame into that engagement. But there is something (oppressive) about a white person who is an authority figure struggling to say your name, because your name is your identity. If they're strug-gling with that, it makes you more conscious of how perhaps your identity doesn't matter. It makes you feel like your identity doesn't matter as much, or it makes you feel othered because you're made aware that you're different because your name is different.

Sometimes, you'd have these well-meaning questions attached to the pronunciation of my name by these author-ity figures. They might say something like, "That's different. Where is that from?" about your name. I found that you often have to justify yourself in ways that perhaps you wouldn't if you just had a straightforward Anglo name, such as where the name comes from or what your cultural roots are. I think the authority figures' interpretation and struggle with saying the name out loud, and the baggage that came along with that, probably overpowered everything for a very long time. I did reach a stage where I would appreciate people appreciating the name, but in the early days, especially when I was younger. I don't know how to articulate it without sounding incredibly cynical, but there were times when my name was framed as an exoticised, fetishised thing by a white person. At the time, I felt almost like I guess the equivalent strongly worded analogy would be like giving a dog a biscuit, petting a dog, and being like, "Nice name". You'd feel happy because you felt somehow validated because you were young. You're still trying to work yourself out and to have validation of any kind from an author-ity figure or someone that you perceive as being in power or in a position of influence that is going to make you feel accepted. If you want to fit in, that's perfect.

What's interesting is if I think back to then, the name change was around my college time. My college was in a predominantly white area on the outskirts of London. It was almost a testing ground to see how an Anglo name would work for me. I was one of very few people of colour in that college at the time. There's more acceptability; you won't have to justify yourself as much as to where you're from, what your cultural values are and who your parents are.

Across my lifetime, I've seen many culturally appropriated names. Let me put it like this: if a white person has an exotic-sounding name, it can be used almost as an accessory. It's just what I've witnessed. I don't claim to speak for anybody, and I may be completely wrong in terms of how that person's lived experience has been, but I know for me to have an exotic-sounding name and to look the way I do that comes with a range of different subtext and meanings. If I were white and called a name that sounded unusual, I don't think I would have to go through quite as much. That's just through observation and the very few experiences I've had which in no way are generalisable, but that's what I've encountered, and I've just found that interesting. To me, that is the ultimate example of identity politics and the idea that because you are privileged when you are white, you can be white, and you can wear long kaftan and your massive linen trousers and be called "India" and that's fine. But you could be from India and dress like that and be brown and maybe be called Bharat, which is Hindi for India, and that might be like, "Foreign alert".

The act of dealing with non-Western names in Western contexts by individuals from the global majority is closely connected to race. This connection is also visible in the way we behave and interact with each other in our daily lives. These attitudes and interactions reflect the colonial legacies and ideologies that shape our self-perception, identity, and desire to assimilate.

Finding Javeria ...

The origin of the name Javeria is Islamic and means "bringer of joy". it was one of the prophet Muhammad's (PBUH) wives' names. The name was given to me because I come from a Muslim family. Traditionally, if you have a child, you will normally give them a Muslim name of a revered figure or someone who had a prominent part to play in Islamic history, so that they may have similar qualities or that they may have similar luck. There's that kind of mentality, so that's where the name came from.

It is pronounced Ja-vaire-eeyaa. I had a white colleague once. (I'm pinpointing the fact that they were white because subconsciously they were percolating a very colonialised idea of working through a "foreign sounding" name by aligning it with a European reference.) They said to me, "It's like Bavaria, the country but with a J. If people can't pronounce it, just do that." I did that for a long time. I didn't really need to, but if I was at the doctor's or at passport control or somewhere where my given name had to be used, I would do that. I did that recently with a friend who is white and specialises in white privilege. She challenged me and said, "Why are you doing that?" She picked me up on it. I was a little taken aback and started reflecting like, "Yeah, she's got a point." It's almost like even by changing my name, I'm secured in that identity, but when I have to use my formal given name in a formal situation, I'm still in that mindset that I probably was in during primary school when I had to find ways of avoiding that embarrassment and justifying. I do like the name now (but) it's difficult to revert to something after more than 20 years. I think at the time when I changed the name, I was subjectively emotionally engaged in a process of wanting to "fit in", whatever that means. As I've grown older and lived my life, I've realised that there is no such thing as fitting in. There are only different layers of performativity. Within the social performativity how much can we be authentic to ourselves? As I've grown older, I realised it's increasingly important to be authentic to oneself, because that's what will keep you grounded. It's decisions you make in your youth which then follow you all the way.

A few years ago I would have categorically said I feel just "Jo", that's me! In recent years, I've felt more split between the two names. I think as I'm getting older, I'm becoming more conscious of my cultural background, origins, race, ethnicity; all these sorts of factors have become more of a prevalent feature to me understanding myself and evolving. In that context, I feel a little bit torn around whether I want to continue using Jo or not, so it's something I have been thinking about very carefully about for a while. I don't know. I think I feel like both, but I feel a bit split across the two because Jo was very much used as a way of fitting in. As I've gotten older, I've realised it doesn't matter if anybody likes or doesn't like my name. If they can't pronounce it, I can tell them how to pronounce it. It shouldn't really be an issue. But I think that self-assurance and strength come with experience and age perhaps. That's been my experience anyway, that it's come with age.

There are some deep-seated issues still there. It depends on what you want to do and where you want to go, really. I think using your given name and being a yoga teacher might be okay because you're in a new age way of thinking and in a different context. But if you want to be a merchant banker or something like that, you might be more likely judged on a complicated name. That's very abstract and it's very speculative. I have no facts to support that comparison but it's just to give an example of how people's world views and the different context can also affect it. Now, I'm thinking how much of that Jo identity really represents me fully, as a whole? I'm going through a little bit of a process in working through all of that. I think I'm still working things out, and going through a process of reflexivity on why I changed my name, what that meant, what it has meant for me to date, going back to my given name, and not using Jo at all, what that would entail? These are all really difficult questions I've been asking myself for a little while now. I'm still processing, I'm still working through them, and I think when I arrived at answers that feel comfortable, then I'll probably have made a decision.

There is always a fear that if I did go back to the name, then it will just be one more thing for someone to be micro-aggressive about and it's already exhausting being a person of colour so I don't know. It's something I'll have to work through in terms of how important it is to me to be authentic in that way if it potentially opens the doors to more racialised traumas. I'm negotiating that in my head. I have dipped my toes in, for example, some of my stuff has J, just J, so it'd be Dr J. Shah rather than Jo. I'm playing around with this idea of J. So, watch the space, don't be too surprised if I evolve into Dr Javeria. It's interesting because when I shared my story with the class, I didn't really think anything of it but now, since this project has been ongoing and (Tony) and I have chatted, it's interesting for me in terms of how I'm processing my name identity.

Returning to Javeria

After much agonising and reflection that morphed into a pandemic-induced existentialist crisis, I finally made the decision to take the plunge and return to my given name. I announced my reversion to Javeria on twitter in 2020 and slowly began transitioning across all my channels, communications, and outputs. Although terrifying at first, the transition wasn't as challenging as I had feared it would be. Possibly because of the issues I was raising earlier on about changes in our national approaches to inclusion and diversity since I was first navigating the name Javeria. The film and working with Tony Giroux on this project have played a significant part in inspiring me to return to my given name and subsequently to finally feel whole in a society that often works so hard at segmenting you into all your different traits and characteristics. I will forever be grateful to this project for aiding those deeply hidden reflections to the surface and giving me the courage to challenge the past and reclaim my name.

Most surprisingly, there has been a genuine appetite amongst the public, my communities, and academia in general to embrace the message of the film and to connect with my story as one of the five other stories shared in the film – but most importantly, to address me by my given name as I wish to be and taking that extra minute to ask me how to pronounce it. The hugest level of support that I have received has been from my primary place of work, the Royal Central School of Speech and Drama, University of London. The institution, my colleagues, and students have been amazing in embracing my identity as Javeria and taking special care to learn to pronounce my name, but also to ensure that my institution-related profile, from my email address to public profile, all reflect the name Javeria. Of course, I still struggle, but the support of networks close to me has meant everything and continued to give me the courage in reclaiming my name and, subsequently, whole identity.

So, if I must end on a note, it would be to not underestimate your power as an ally to someone going through a journey like mine. That one genuine attempt at getting it right, at really seeing someone in their name, that one gesture of respect, can make such a huge difference in giving someone struggling with name identity a sense of belonging.

Applying Whiteness ecology theory to Javeria's story

Chronosystem

My life as a British Asian Muslim woman is deeply influenced by my father's immigration as a "Commonwealth subject" to the UK in the 1960s. Being a first-generation immigrant child, I was born and raised during the political era of Thatcher's Britain and the unstable racial politics of modern-day UK society. As I entered adulthood, I had to face the aftermath of the 9/11 attacks, which led to an increase in anti-Muslim sentiments.

Macrosystem and exosystem

In society, certain dominant ideologies prevailed that had a negative impact on my experiences. One of these ideologies was deliberately excluding Britain's colonial history from mainstream discussions. This resulted in a biased and racist narrative surrounding the migration of Windrush and Pakistani people to the UK during the 1950s and 1960s, which was not appropriately contextualised. This manifested in an ideological and mass media representational dynamic that mocked and vilified Black and Brown communities through negative stereotypes or stratifying policymaking. Underpinning this was the synonymising of Britishness with Whiteness. Despite being born in the UK, I am still asked where I am from to this day, and there is an insistence to explain where I'm really from because a Brown body couldn't possibly be British.

Mesosystem and microsystem
Javeria's attempts at assimilating into a Whiteness ecology

My story spans over two decades and reflects the complexity of navigating a non-Western name in UK contexts. Complex navigations that lead to an identity crisis and a want to assimilate, or as the teen Javeria/Jo would have phrased, "wanting to fit in". It was a journey that brought me back full circle to my original name, as I realised over time that complete assimilation and acceptance would never be possible for me in the context of race and ethnicity. That all a drive for assimilation was doing was moving me deeper into performatives of identification that were deemed as socially acceptable. That acceptability was deeply rooted in normative Whiteness and Eurocentrism.

I could never have assimilated and been accepted into the very structures and systems designed to exclude me. I can change my name, but I can't change the colour of my skin. I can make invisible my faith, but I can't change my ethnicity or cultural heritage. These realisations have brought me full circle to my initial identity, but this time, to embrace, reclaim, and perhaps most importantly, accept it rather than reject or reframe it for the comfort of others.

3
My name is Dheeraj

Exploring name identity in the context of ethnicity and the acting profession

- Readers interpret Dheeraj's story using Whiteness ecology to understand name navigation in the context of ethnicity and the acting profession.
- Drama educators and industry leaders are motivated to reflect on their academic and professional practices relating to names to facilitate inclusive acting cultures.

Introduction

This is Dheeraj's story, which you can also see in the associated *My Name Is* film. Dheeraj is a British Indian actor and, in his story, he talks about the challenges of navigating a non-Western name as an actor in training. Dheeraj also contextualises his story in the context of accents and diaspora.

The past

My most vivid memory is of the school register and any new or substitute teacher and being like, "D-Dur-Dee", and then I'll be like, "Dheeraj", and I couldn't say it. Usually, I would say "Dee-raj", but I would never say "Dee-rij". It would always be "Dee-raj", so I'd cut out the H because it made it easier for people who aren't from South Asian communities to understand the name. When I was younger, there was a certain level of dread when people read out the first and second names because it'd be like, I don't know, Alex Dilly, Ellie Roberts. Then it comes to me, and it'd be like, "Dee… Dee-raj… Ah…" and I would often have to step in and say, "Oh, Dheeraj Ahluwalia" – and then even the teacher would say it back in a way that was not malicious or to be funny or to take the mick.[1] They'd be trying to say, "Ah-loo-wal-ya", and then I would giggle because it would be an awkward thing and whatnot. So, I think there was a certain level of dread that used to form around people saying my name. My second name, Ahluwalia, is tricky to pronounce; people would say it in weird ways, like "Hulu-alia", or even use words of profanity inserted into the name, as you can imagine kids would do, right? But I think, in general, maybe the fact that my cultural background was being mocked, even if it was done in a friendly way, identifying as Dhee was made subconsciously because I didn't want to say "Dheeraj" and identified more as Indian as that would allow me to be targeted more for racism. So, there may be some filter in there that I did not know.

I had some weird ones because my name is spelt D-H-E-E-R-A-J. So, the H throws people off. So, people are "De-Dheeraj" or "Durj". Some people just wholly can't say it, so they'll be like "Durj". I was given the nickname Dhee very early. My parents started to call me Dhee, as a nickname. So, by the time I got to 16, 17, and 18 in my school, all my teachers called me Dhee. There wasn't a teacher who called me Dheeraj. I think it's always a two-way process as I accept or even say, "Oh, just call me Dhee, that's fine, that's what everyone calls me anyway." But it is also easier. I can't remember any figure of authority taking the time to pronounce my name. None of the teachers could say my name, and none of them could remember my name either. So, I will almost always self-censor. I won't try and get them to understand it. I wouldn't correct them. I would help them by shortening my name, which is weird when you think about it. Really, it shouldn't be the case at all. I shouldn't have to be shortening my name for the sake of someone else.

It is a case of when I say my name is Dheeraj, and they understand this straight away, then it's almost like we've already broken through a few of the barriers it takes to get to know someone.

Acting

When I first joined my first acting school, I used my full name, Dheeraj Ahluwalia, and then, for the first term of acting, they would read off the name, and I noticed that no one could say my name. Then, in my acting school, I said, "Oh, you can just call me Dhee." It was a big thing in acting to decide to go with the name, you know, Dhee instead of Dheeraj. And I was also battling with that because of so much of my identity; I feel more comfortable when people call me Dheeraj than when they call me Dhee. Because Dhee is a nickname, I don't feel as strongly connected to the name as Dheeraj because my parents and grandparents mostly call me Dheeraj. I don't know, though, but it's also, as actors as well when we do accents, it's almost that when you say Dheeraj, it may be hard to pronounce for someone that isn't familiar with the Indian dialect because obviously, it would be "Dee-rij", which is a more Indian way of saying it. If you can't pronounce it correctly, then you feel stupid. In the same way, if I do an accent I'm not strong in, I feel like I sound dumb when I try to say a name in an Eastern European accent because I can't do an Eastern European accent. Do you know what I mean?

Although you would love for them to judge you on talent and stuff like that, especially in our industry, I feel like how people remember you really matters. And subtle things like them not remembering your name don't factor into the big decision. They won't be like, "I'm not taking him on because I can't say his name", but it does factor into a tiny bit of that. That little bit is essential.

Uber for Dheeraj?

It's such a complicated thing, though, because I grew up here. And I identify as British, right? I don't speak Hindi; I don't speak Panjabi. I don't speak my mother tongue per se. Now that I'm older, I'm embracing my culture way more. But I think, significantly growing up in a Caucasian context, being British was more accessible than being Indian, so I never really bat an eyelid about saying that my name is Dhee. I should introduce myself more as Dhee and anglicise my name, Dheeraj. But again, it depends on who I talk to really.

I was born in the UK, worlds apart from India, but then, it's hard to work out which is more important. There isn't one that is more important. They both feed into each other, but there is something that feels more whole when I think about Indian culture.

I don't know if that is just because it's so removed from me. You know, people always want to be associated with something different or something almost mysterious, or that I am Indian, and there are not many Indians here or whatever. I don't know. I feel more comfortable being called Dheeraj, but I'd like to know if that has anything to do with my heritage or just because that's the proper name I've been given.

If I'm speaking to someone I presume to be Indian, South Asian, or Pakistani, I always say my name is Dheeraj. That's the name I give. If they're not from that culture, I automatically say Dhee. I never say Dheeraj. It's one of those things, but I don't know. It's not that I'm ashamed of it.

Interestingly, if I introduce myself as Dhee to someone from a South Asian background, they'd be like, "What is that short for?" If I say my name is Dhee to someone who has no link to a South Asian background or doesn't know much about it, they will never ask me, "What's that short for?" They would think that's my name, Dhee, which is interesting. This is why, probably now, I say, "My name is Dheeraj" to South Asian people because I know that they know Dhee is not my full name. If I say my name is Dhee, I'll get accused of being a coconut, right? They'll think I'm just trying to anglicise my name because I think I'm British and I'm not Indian. So, I'll always say Dheeraj in that case. They know my name is Dheeraj if they're of Asian heritage. I will have an instant connection and rapport with them. And I think that's because it's almost like, "Oh, you understand my culture or the culture I grew up in because you can say my name properly", which is a weird litmus test for that because obviously, someone could not say your name correctly, but also completely understand your cultural heritage straight away.

There are Uber drivers that will be able to say my name straight away. "Uber for Dheeraj?" There is a feeling of being more comfortable straight away because they can say my name, and there are times when they will be like, "Oh, how do I say that name? How do I pronounce it?" And you will spend 30 seconds talking about how to pronounce the name. And then we'll start to talk about India and heritage and all that stuff. So, yeah, some people take the time. Teachers never did, I don't think. Not really.

Reflections

For someone to ask me, "What was your name? Dheeraj?" be curious and ask, "Sorry, where's that from?" Or trying to pronounce it. That feels good to me; it's nice that they're taking the time, but it takes a certain level of confidence to do that. People are generally quite shy and awkward and would almost think, "It's rude if I asked about his name. So let me pretend I know it even though I don't." It would be nice if people took more time because you're trying to understand me more, which I'm never going to think is rude.

It's difficult because I used to think about first impressions and how little nuances of behaviour can cause an openness in interaction or a barrier. And I see that when I introduce myself as Dhee, and they get the name straight away, they almost feel more comfortable interacting with me because they can remember the name. "Oh Dhee!" you know, "blah blah blah." Whereas if

I say Dheeraj, it's like, "What?" "Dheeraj. Dheeraj." I know they're not going to remember that name instantly, and because of that, there is an enormous subconscious barrier between them and me. For example, if I can't remember someone's name, I don't want to be like, "Sorry, what was your name again?" I'd rather be able to say, "Oh hey, Tony, or Bill, or whatever" when I'm interacting with them. If I can't remember their name, there is an automatic barrier being put up because I can't interact with them as I would have liked to. So, if I say "Dheeraj" and they don't understand, and if it's a quick interaction or there's no time to be like, "Sorry?", there's no time to be curious about the name, so I think it does put a barrier up, and people just forget. They don't even want to ask me again because they figured they're going to be rude or say it wrong, which can come across as even more disrespectful. If someone took the time to understand my name, I wouldn't think it wasn't pleasant. I would think it's more polite. I think it's a nice thing for them to do, which is interesting because I sometimes feel that I can't do that with other people.

Two sides to me

It is two sides of me. Dheeraj is the more Indian and the more homely side. It feels more, I don't know, like the essence of me if I can be so brave to use such a broad term, but yeah, it does feel more like me. And Dhee is the exterior. Or rather than it being more British or Indian, I feel like Dhee is the exterior that I present to people to make them understand. Dhee is the more accessible version of me. Does that make sense? The more accessible version of me is Dhee, and then Dheeraj is the more innate, who I am, side of me – but then again, it's vulnerable when I say, "My name is Dheeraj" and people don't remember it. It almost feels awkward, or like there's a certain level of … not shame. Shame isn't the right word, but there is something in it if I say my name and people don't get it immediately. There's a certain level of retracting in myself and being like, "Oh, that doesn't feel nice." If you get what I mean, it almost feels like they're making fun of the name in some ways.

It's a difficult one. Part of it is that I say my name is Dhee because it just eases the interaction, making it easier for them to remember my name and interact with me. But I guess part of it also is that saying the name Dheeraj may be more like me and maybe a bit more vulnerable in a certain way.

Perceived shifts in British attitudes towards ethnicity and race

My parents went through so much racism, and with their names experienced that people were not taking the time because that's something they were not willing to do. For example, my adoptive parents' names are Satbir and Jagjit, whereas they go by Sats and Jag. So, they shortened it as well. My dad, grew up in Manchester, and had huge issues with bullying because of his race. So that was probably more of an "I'm going to shorten it because people don't have the willingness to accept me as my full Indian name, and Sats sounds more anglicised."

However, because I haven't experienced such intense levels of resistance based on my colour, it is more of a confidence thing now. I don't know. That's just based on my experience. I think it differs, but my lens on it is that because I know if someone explained, for example, a Russian name, which has been done many times and I don't get it the first two times, it's not a sense of me being unwilling to learn their name or to accept their heritage. It's more than, "Oh, no. Now, I feel bad. I don't want to ask again because I don't want to be rude", or "I don't want them to feel like I don't understand", or "I didn't get it the first time", or "I wasn't listening." So it can be more of a confidence thing.

The future

I often think about my kids' names. When I have kids, what are they going to be called? I want to give them a name that is easily said. I want it to be easy to remember, and I want it not to be complicated. I know that someone can easily oppose that by saying, "It's all about culture, and it's all about embracing your culture, and you shouldn't have to filter yourself or anyone" – but I genuinely believe in this day when it comes to something like a name which is your identity, I feel like you can still have that identity in that cultural background whilst also having a name that is easy to pronounce.

Some part of me feels like I'm just being pedantic if I insist that people call me Dheeraj. I don't know. You can say Dheeraj if you want. That's okay. Or you can contact me, Dhee, that's okay. I don't know if it's necessary to say, "No, you have to call me Dheeraj." How do you navigate that relationship? I don't know because it's complicated. It's about respect, saying the name right, and trying to say it exactly. Everyone should take the time to say Dheeraj correctly. I was coerced into calling myself Dhee because people couldn't know it, and no one took the time to say it. I could have gone down that route, but for me, this situation is so complicated just because I identify with both and understand both sides. I don't know how to navigate it. I don't know whether saying Dhee is me filtering myself for others or if I am genuinely doing that because I don't care. I think it's easier if you call me Dhee because we build that connection straight away. So, it's such a complex situation.

Applying Whiteness ecology to a backdrop of messy colonial histories of migration and nationality

Dheeraj's story provides insight into the issues surrounding non-Western name navigation in a British context. His reference to his parents' experiences with name navigation as first-generation migrants to the UK is more racially charged in comparison to Dheeraj's experiences, which have also been complex but subtle – indicating that racism in the UK still exists but has become subtle in its articulations over time. Dheeraj's experiences of initially using his given name and then anglicising it due to the inability of teachers being able to pronounce his name speaks to issues surrounding actor training and prompts me to ask why the pronunciation of Dheeraj is so challenging in a training landscape where complex White European names such as Stanislavsky, Meisner or Chekhov are pronounced with ease?

Dheeraj's educational experiences echo mine. We see a pattern emerging here in how much of the global majorities from the British post-colonial diaspora are made to feel invisible and unworthy because of a lack of effort by their teachers when it comes to the pronunciation of their names. In both Dheeraj's and my case, we anglicised our names to assimilate and for the ease of others, but is this fair to the student?

At undergraduate and postgraduate levels, the UK actor training landscape is strongly connected to the performing arts and film industries and aims to prepare students for work. Considering this context, it is worth considering ways the actor training class-room and, subsequently, the industry can be made more inclu-sive through racial and cultural literacy. A starting point for the training classroom would be something as small as trying to learn how to pronounce a student's name correctly. For the industry, it would be to consider cultural nuances relating to groups in the representations they curate in front of the screen and stage and the expansion of diversity behind the scenes so that individuals don't feel pressured to assimilate to colonial ideological norms at the cost of losing their authentic selves.

4
My name is Pereko

Exploring the significance of name identity in the context of pronunciation and racial and colonial contexts

- To facilitate readers' interpretation of Pereko's story within the context of pronunciation and racial and colonial circumstances.
- To facilitate understanding of the negative impact of mispronouncing someone's name on individuals.

Introduction

Originally from South Africa, Pereko studies and lives in London. Her name story captures the racial tensions in navigating her name and identity in South Africa, alluding to the region's challenging histories with racial apartheid and white supremacy. Pereko's story then shifts to navigating her name identity in the UK and the separate challenges this has brought up for her. While Pereko's experiences are varied across both contexts, she can consolidate these experiences to share some everyday learning and recommendations for the readers' consideration.

Growing up in South Africa

My name is Pereko; it's not even common in South Africa. I grew up in Johannesburg, South Africa. That's where I lived for most of my life. It's a big mix of cultures, but it depends on where you live. Because I come from a middle-class family, I managed to stay in the suburbs, so I stayed in our community. We were probably one of the few black families on the road a couple of years ago.

My name has affected my life to some extent, explicitly growing up with South African politics. In South Africa, racism is still a genuine thing. This is such a ridiculous example, but it's the reality: if you're booking a place, let's say, whether it's a hotel or you're looking at a restaurant, and I say my name is Sarah and I book, it might be easy for me to get a booking at a particular place. If I say, "Hi, my name is Pereko, I would like to book", they might say, "Sorry, it's full." That's an actual thing. That's not made up; that's a real thing that happens. So simply because I can change my accent, sound more Western, and call myself Sarah, I might get a booking for a place easier, which is interesting in 2019.

In terms of any other impacts on my life, I guess it's simply because maybe it's a challenging name for people to say. The way it rolls and sounds, or because it's not a well-known name. Because I interacted and socialised with many people of colour in Johannesburg, they say it (my name) correctly. Maybe it might be a little often in terms of intonation, but there are a lot of African cultures in South Africa so that people might be like, "Oh, Pereko. I've never heard that name; that's an interesting name." Because it's not a very trendy name, not many people know it or have it. It's not even a common name in South Africa. Not at all. I've only known one other person with my name, so …

When I was in high school, I used to anglicise my name a little bit, probably because it was a predominantly white school. Even now, many people don't say my name correctly, but I've seen that they've given it a shot. This is how they will say my name, so at least it's not something like, "Oh, can we call you?" or, "Oh, let's call you?" because that happened in high school.

Pk. That's what many people know me as; some still call me that, and I'm trying to remove that from me and the way they interact with me. I thought like I had to almost "englishify" my name. I have learned a couple of nicknames, but those are more personal; they come from a different space, but at that time, it was in high school, it was kind of just like, "Oh, don't you have another name or what's your nickname or can we just call you this" like a million people threw that, slapped that name on me and from then there was no turning back so, I'm very particular with what I like to be called and that's my name.

Pereko, that's the South African version of it. It didn't carry as much weight (for me) as it does now as a person who is older (in relation to) my identity and the politics that come with it. I think with my experiences and the older you get and the more you witness, what is at the forefront is that I'm a person of colour, I'm South African, and I'm black, and my name, and how difficult it is, and the politics that come with it – all of the elements of who you are come into play so as a child, I don't remember much of that being an issue with me. I don't know if it was an acceptance thing. Just so it was easier for them, for white people, or they feel like I'm closer to them because high school was a bizarre time for me, for a lot of black people who are in a predominantly white space simply because we could afford to be there. Because we could feel wildly shoved to the side if we're a person of colour in a predominantly white space than in South Africa, where there are tons of black people.

Significance of my name

It's a Tswana name; Tswana is like a language. My family originates from South Africa. I have other parts of my family from Botswana, like on the corner of South Africa, just north of South Africa. So, my grandfather on my dad's side gave me the name. It's from an aunt I have never met before; I think it's related to work, but I can't say what element of work or whether it's a hard worker. But it stems from that because to work is Mereko, so it's just with an M. But my name is Pereko.

Carrying my identity in my name

Wherever I am, wherever I go, (my name) is a part of my identity and an extension of my roots and where I come from. It's part of my being as a person because I like to think I'm a hard worker, and I hope that one day I will reap the benefits of that, which I believe many African people want to do regarding naming their kids. So, if they feel like this will be the direction you're taking your life, whatever they try and name you based on where they see your future taking you. So, I think in terms of that, yeah. It carries weight for me; it's more than just a name. It's more than a couple of letters flanked together and thrown at you, thrown at a person. It's almost like the prospect of where your life will take you and what they hope for you. You are usually named by an elder, not just your parents. Your parents might have a say in it, but whether it's grandparents or something like that, they will give you a name. So, I have a first name, middle name, and surname, and I think it all flows into your being and not the fate of your life but the direction you'll take that will hopefully be positive.

Now, I think I'm older and more aware of things, I'm like, "No", this is how my name should be said. Whether speaking in English or another language, I will always tell my name as Pereko. You must figure it out wherever and whichever environment I'm in.

Navigating name identity

I didn't used to, but I've grown to like my name. Now I love it, so I appreciate it, and I think it carries weight because wherever I am, my name will always be Pereko. Right now, I'm living in London. I didn't know I'd be here, but here I am; it's a very foreign place to me and has its ups and downs. It's not home, but I feel like with me and my name, I carry; this is so cringe, but with me and my name, I have my home with it. I'm in a different (head) space and environment, and I would like people to try to say my name. So, that's the energy I'm coming with. I know it just requires a bit more work from my side because many people here haven't been exposed to a name like mine. But if I can say your name or try, you should be able to tell my name or at least try.

People have asked if there's something that I would prefer being called, but not necessarily beyond that; like, if I say no, then they can accept it, but other people have been like, "Oh, what's your English name or what's your white name?" and I was like, I don't have any English name or white name. If I say my name is Pereko, but you can call me whoever, that's different. If you ask me what my name is, and I tell you my name is Pereko, it's because I want you to call me Pereko. You know what I mean? So, if I'm not giving you any nickname or anything else, that sounds like your problem, not mine.

Sometimes people ask, "Oh, where is she from?" Do you know what I mean? "Where do I box you? Where do you fit in the world?" But I always find that interesting, more positive than not, because people are a bit more curious to know who you are, how you ended up here, or your story, which is usually more positive than not. So, it's been positive because then sometimes people are more curious to ask you questions, interested in getting to know you, which I always think is excellent in a place like London where a lot of the time people seem like they don't have the time or they are unbothered to interact with other people that they might have never met before or might not speak to in general, simply because they have things to do.

It's a mix of both. If they end up saying "Pereko", then maybe say it slower, like "Pereko", so they can hear the sound. And then other times people are just like, "Pereko", okay, and then whether it is right or wrong, they're just too unbothered to figure out whether that's okay, whether they could do better for themselves regarding how they say my name. Because sometimes, people are in a rush or unbothered.

Now I'm older and just more aware of things. And I'm like, no, this is how my name is supposed to be said. Whether I speak English or whichever language I speak, I will always tell my name as Pereko. Wherever and whichever environment I'm in, you'll just have to try and figure it out.

It makes a difference in terms of how I interact with that person or how I see that person because if we're going often just meeting people, that's the first impression like, what's your name, or whatever. So, just going off that, let's say, makes a bit of a difference, but what I try to do is if someone rushes it over, I'll tell my name again, so just repeat it. It'd be like, no, Pereko. So, that has become my responsibility. If people say it correctly the first time, that's even better or even closer because some people here seem to think it sounds like I'm saying it in Spanish or something, and I'm like, no, it's just an African name. When people pay more attention, it's lovely and endearing because it means "I see you." It's almost like a form of recognition. It's like, "I see you, you see me", we can go from there.

Importance of names

I think it's important to have pride in your name and to want to learn or know about other people here, understanding why would you not be curious to learn where their roots are, where they come from, what their lineage or whatever it might be? That's the most exciting thing about people, societies, and diversities. It's just like it broadens your horizon more than you can imagine.

My closing note would be that it's essential for us as people to know a name isn't just a name; it carries a lot, more so for some people than others. So I think it's good to acknowledge that and recognise that and try and practice saying people's names correctly every day in your daily life; you never know who might be necessary, who might play a significant role in your life, who might not, but that shouldn't be any reason why we try to recognise people, acknowledge people, and say their name.

Whiteness ecology in a still colonial context

The part of Pereko's story that reflects her time in South Africa represents the colonially driven marginalisation with an active pressure to assimilate to Whiteness norms. Pereko makes several comments that reflect white supremacy in action when she discusses the neighbourhoods, high schools, politics, and barriers to accessibility based on name, accent, and racial make-up. In sharing her South African roots and name context, we can better understand Pereko's determination to maintain the authenticity of her name in its pronunciation and use, as it represents so much more than just a name for her.

Her experiences in London, while perhaps not as extreme as the ones cited in South Africa, are still problematic on many levels. For example, the expectation for her to shorten her name or to be asked directly what her "white name" is are also shocking occurrences that represent the filtering down of everyday racism that Whiteness ecology theory presents. The key learning that we should be taking away from Pereko's story is that names can often carry many meanings, histories, and significance for the individuals we encounter. We should not expect those who are already marginalized to accommodate our lack of cultural and racial understanding; this expectation is deeply disrespectful rather than emphasizing our ease of pronunciation. It can leave scars on the individual who may be at the receiving end of our subconscious ignorance. For this reason, we must encourage educators to recruit or assign students from different cultural backgrounds to prepare a little in their knowledge of each student's context and advance their socio-political contextual knowledge and cultural literacies.

5
My name is Sahil

Exploring the significance of name identity in the context of pronunciation and cultural context

- To invite readers to interpret Sahil's story to understand name navigation in the context of pronunciation and cultural context.
- To facilitate understanding of individual's potential reconciliations with their name being mispronounced.

Introduction

Of Panjabi Indian heritage, Sahil grew up in New Zealand and spoke to us while studying as an international student in London. In his story, Sahil shares the challenges surrounding the correct pronunciation of his name in different professional and social contexts and how he has learnt to adjust and navigate different spaces to protect his peace.

About me

My name is Sahil. I'm a Hindu, and I was born in India and moved to New Zealand when I was around seven. I'm from Panjab, which is a state in the north of India. The people from the area are commonly called Panjabis. I'm from Ludhiana, a state known for textiles and manufacturing. I only remember a little of being in India with my grandparents and close family. Most of my life has been in New Zealand, but there's still that Indian upbringing and culture ingrained in me from my parents. So yeah, it's still like recalling going back to India every so often, every couple of years, to chat with family.

So, in New Zealand, I live in Auckland, the biggest city in New Zealand. Auckland is multicultural. We pride ourselves on that. I think there are over 100 nationalities residing in Auckland alone, especially since the 1990s when there was a massive immigration boom. So, you got Indians, Sri Lankans, Bangladeshis, Filipinos, Chinese, Japanese, and Koreans. What else would you have? Taiwanese people, Indonesians, and you got the Europeans, like the whole European continent, staying there as well. Many people come here to retire as well, and then some come to New Zealand for a holiday, love the place so much, and decide to stay, which is interesting. So yeah, it's multicultural and diverse, like London.

Growing up

I went to a predominantly white private school where there was little to no interaction and representation of other cultures, although I wasn't the only Indian kid in my school. You also had the native people, the islanders like the Māori, there. So, there was a good mixture of those two ethnicities. Not that many Indians and not that many Asians then, but that's slowly started to change. And there's more of us, a lot more Asian representation now in New Zealand. Currently, it is like a multi-hybrid; you're mixing in with the New Zealand identity, your cultural upbringing, and your parents, which is your Asian heritage. It's a good mixture, and in a way, it's also a bit of a privilege. It's exciting. That's the way I see it.

Name experiences

When I was working, my boss kept getting my name wrong, and he's a very senior guy in the business. I think I corrected him once. I was like, "Sahil". And he's a very old guy, and he's like, "No". He kept saying Saheel, and I said, "Okay, well, listen, I'm just not going to bother trying to correct this guy." I've already told him once, and then I felt shy talking about it, fearing any repercussions, drawbacks, or issues arising in our professional relationship. He just continued, but that was just him and his personality. That's the kind of guy he was. He's an ancient school and resistant to change. So, he's got his cultural values, and that's the kind of guy he was, which I didn't take offence to. You meet different types of people in life; some people can adapt, and others reach a certain point where they're willing or unwilling to adapt. For him, it's a tiny thing. Other people in the business fully got my name and pronounced it correctly.

I'll tell you another story: when I was working in a call centre trying to get extra cash, I thought, "Well, I got to sell newspapers online over the phone to these people to get them onto the subscription." Now, I can't say my real name, Sahil, and the connotation behind that is that "Oh, this is a foreign person calling me in, and I'm less inclined to buy from them." So, I just used to say, "Hi, my name is Simon." To get through and make it more relatable to the individual. That was a lot easier for people to swallow because other people in the call centre also used to do that. After all, when you're over the phone, you don't know who's on the other line, but the only thing you know about them is their name. And through that name, you think of the person's looks and interests. You put these stereotypes in your brain, and it's like, "Well, let's reverse that. Let's give them a reason to buy the paper and make me more money while I'm in university." It worked because I think I was the top sales-person in my first week. So, it just really helped me out financially.

It wasn't because I was "ashamed" of my name or anything like that; it's more like being thoughtful about your environment and owning what you know about yourself and what you know about other people and their sort of perceptions of immigrants (even though I wouldn't consider myself an immigrant, I would consider myself a Kiwi more than anything). So, you kind of play to that environment. It's up to the individual. I could have been a social justice warrior and kept correcting customers, saying, "No, it's Sahil." And they're like, "Oh, Sahil, not Saheel", which creates a hurdle, a barrier and makes it challenging to try and sell a paper. It's just that you have to play to your environment. That's what I learned from that. That's what I take on board because some-times there's no point in correcting the individual. After all, there's nothing to gain from it. So, you're only going to meet them for two seconds. So, let's carry on, you know.

You create a barrier when you're over the phone trying to assert the pronunciation of your name because they don't have the time. It's purely from a business point of view. You're trying to sell something and want to build rapport immediately over the phone. And from that point of view, it's essential to create as few barriers as possible between you and the individual. But in an interaction from day to day, which is a lot more personal, there's no sort of business aspect involved. It's just you are being you. It's essential to be authentic and own what you have. You know what I mean? That's the way I see it and the way I take it. Yeah, because you're not trying to sell anything. You're not trying to create some fake relationship for the sake of business, or you have to get yourself through university. It's just you are being you, owning up to yourself, and identifying with what you are. And that's how I take it from a personal interaction instead of over the phone. It's just about being smart about it. It's different from my name; everybody should get it right. It's more like, "Well, the people that need to get it right need to get it. The people that don't matter, as per se. I don't matter to them. Why try to exert something that is not important to them." That's the way I take it. It is more like playing to your circumstance; that's how I see it.

For example, I remember working at Orion Health and dealing with some senior people. These were like 20–30 years my seniors in experience and partners in the firm, and they're like, "Saheel". I didn't feel comfortable correcting a partner who's been working here for 40 years while I'm just starting – but as I got towards the end of my tenure at EY or Orion Health, it's more like, "No, this is who I am. I need to own up to it. This is my name, and if they're getting it wrong, I have the right to correct my name." So, it's taking more ownership of that. I think that's a battle that you kind of face growing up. When you're younger, you're a bit hesitant to assert yourself or correct your name because you don't want to offend the other person, but I think a lot of people take that with respect. In hindsight, it's like, "Okay, yeah, you value your name. I will make sure that I make more of a conscious effort to pronounce it correctly." That's how I would interpret it, and I'm sure many other people will hopefully do the same.

Meaning of my name

A beautiful bank side by the river, that's what Sahil means. One of the priests would have given me the name, and the priest would have been like, "Yeah, this is a set of names, and pick one or something." I don't know. That's how it went, but I'm not sure. This was a very different cultural period in India, though it still happens quite often.

My name reflects the culture and upbringing that both parents gave me and what I've been exposed to growing up. I'm more respectful of the upbringing that I have had, the religion that I'm part of, and the culture that my family has provided and that I've been a part of. That's where I get a sense of pride and joy and respect. This name is just the narrowing down of all of that. I am very grateful for the name my parents gave me, but it's not like that's me, and my name is me. I don't think of it like that. There's more to me than just my name at the end of the day.

Pronouncing my name

Initially, I didn't use to assert my name because I didn't take it as too big of a deal. It was not something I thought of as a do-or-die, but I realised that people were not saying it correctly as I got older. It got to me eventually because this is who I am, a big part of me. It's just showing respect to the individual when you can get their name correct. Then I was like, "Okay, no, I need to be more assertive about my name, respect my upbringing, and let other people know." It's more about coming to terms with your name and your identity and then being able to share it respectfully.

Your first interaction with people when they hear your name and aren't familiar with it creates a barrier between you, if only for a few seconds. If I were to say it how my grandparents say it or how my mom used to say it before she moved to New Zealand, it would be Saa-hill, which has a little Indian twang in there, but yeah, out in public, people are like, Sahil or some people don't even say it correctly. I know it's not on purpose, but sometimes you don't correct them.

Well, my name is Sahil. And then they're like, "Oh, sorry, what?" And I'm like Sa-Hill. So, I have to break it down for them, especially during the initial interaction with people. That's what I feel uncomfortable doing initially. It was a bit hard, but that's what I have to do: break it down for people because they tend to go away without knowing me and just read the name. They're like Saheel, and I'm like, "It's not Saheel. It's Sahil." So yeah, I'm breaking it down into syllables, just like I must. Sahil: Sahil. Sa-heel is another one, but it is mainly like Sehil. It's pretty easy to pronounce, to be honest, but Sahil is usually the one they typically get wrong, and it's like, no, it's not Sehil. There's a Sa and a hill. So that's the way I break it down for them. Some people do it subconsciously. I'm fully aware it's not a conscious effort for them to get it wrong; it's subconscious and not malicious in any way, shape, or form. That's fine, I understand. Understanding that they're not trying to enter a conflict or cause you harm. For me, as an individual, it's about taking ownership and feeling comfortable then. For example, in a public setting, you don't want to correct the individual in front of a group of 20 other people, but maybe you do, so those are the decisions you will make as an individual. Do I tell them now, or do I tell them in private? And you have to be aware of that as well. Like there's a time and place to correct somebody, I also keep that in the back of my mind.

I find it easy being in the presence of people if they get my name wrong first because it's not too hard to correct. I interacted with people who couldn't get my name right the first time because they were receptive and open to learning how to pronounce it correctly. I never feel the pressure that I have to assert myself. It's more like there's a willingness from their side as well, in general. Most people are good with it. They wait for me to say my name and say, "Okay. Yeah, that's how you pronounce it." But in general, most people pick up on it due to the mixture of ethnicities here in London and Auckland. It's Sahil. I wouldn't say it's too tricky, so I don't have to go around clarifying to many people all the time, but I think once I say it once or twice, people tend to get the gist. It's pretty easy to pick up.

In general, I can correct people infrequently. That's great, but it's all about how I assert myself: "No, this is how you pronounce the name." And if I say it pleasantly or respectably where I respect my name, people see that. And I think they appreciate that. And then they make more of an effort to remember how I said my name instead of "No. It's Sahil; it doesn't matter if he doesn't get his name right."

So, it's not the end of the world. But if it were going further, if it was constantly getting it wrong intentionally and messing it up, I would be more inclined to say, "No, you got to get it right. I've been working with you for over a year, and now it's time for you to sort it out." I've gotten better at it now. Like if it's acquaintances, I still try to correct them. If they get it wrong, I say very clearly again, this is my name. And I know they do it unintentionally because you just met the guy, so it's not a big deal. But with close friends, all my close mates know how to pronounce my name.

It's all about how I take ownership of my name and present it to them. I'm proud of what I am. They see that, and then they reciprocate, ensuring they get it right the next time they say my name. So, it's all about that as opposed to me being very clumsy and very shy about it. Then, it's a different scenario. Then it's like, "Well, if you can't try to get your name right, then it's alright for me not even to make an effort." I think that sometimes, subconsciously, that may go through the person's head, there is a slight hesitancy, you know. There will always be a slight awkwardness because there's a subtle cultural barrier between two people, but it's all about how willing I am to show them how to pronounce my name. It all depends on me to a certain extent. I don't take pride in what I'm saying and if I'm going to be quite shy and introverted about it, then there's no real impetus for them to process that into their brain. So, it's all about me, just making sure I pronounce my name clearly. That's how I feel. After I've said it one or two times, I think it's on the other person to receive that, interpret it, bring it back out, and just be able to pronounce it correctly because it's there. And if they can't and are apologetic about it, then I'm happy to repeat it. It's not a big deal because if I can say it correctly and get their name right, then it's mutual respect.

It's not hard; there are many more complex names, but this is two syllables, so it's not much of a challenge. I have met other people out there who might have a complicated name, and I'm going to butcher it up the first time I meet them completely, and

I want to be like, "Sorry, what?" But then they're going to repeat it, and twice or three times, I'm like, "Okay, cool. I got it, thank you." So, I make sure I get their name right. Instead of pretending I got it right the first time, I heard it and just tried to skate around their name and mumble it instead. So, if that's how I want to be treated, then I must be able to do the same for them as well.

As for my surname, they've said it quite correctly. It's not too different from the aurora you see at the North Pole, so they resonate with that, and it's a similar sort of pronunciation, so they're fine. Yeah, it's similar. So, it's like, "Okay, cool. You got it right. It's like Aurora."

Compromising in Whiteness ecology

Sahil's experience highlights the complexities of code-switching between various identities based on different names, including aliases. It also involves choosing which battles to fight when it comes to correct name pronunciation. As Sahil shares, there were instances where he adopted Western names to facilitate communication during his telesales job. Or when he corrected a senior manager who continued to mispronounce his name, he stopped correcting him and accepted the mispronunciation. Sahil reflects an adaptive and sometimes assimilative approach to his name navigations; however, he represents a clear sense of pride and connection with his name. Sahil represents what individuals can come under when navigating non-Western names in Western contexts and provides tools for those in a similar position to him to manage different contexts and environments. While Sahil recognises the challenges and barriers and is very generous in compromising, he also asserts his boundaries based on context. For example, as he says, he would expect those close to him to pronounce his name correctly. There are also parallels between Pereko and Sahil's stories in that they both strongly associate their names with their cultural heritage. In Pereko's case, this is South Africa, and in Sahil's, it is the Panjab. Sahil's heritage references two distinctly different colonial contexts of India and New Zealand, which may inform his approaches to code-switching and recognising yet accepting the white privilege he encounters relating to the mispronunciation of his name.

Sahil's story teaches us that, ideally, individuals shouldn't feel they must hide elements of their identity to be accepted. What measures can we implement so individuals do not feel pressured to code-switch between their authentic and assimilated selves? Let us normalise name pronunciation tools, for example, to support the learning and correct pronunciation of names.

6
My name is Armen

Exploring the significance of claiming name identity in the context of negative past experiences

- To invite readers to interpret Armen's story to understand name navigation in the context of social change.
- To facilitate understanding of individual's potential reconciliations with their name identity over time.

Introduction

A Londoner with Armenian heritage, Armen gives us insights into how name navigation has changed. Armen introduces us to an intersectional insight into his name journey through the lens of class and ethnicity. He shares difficult childhood experiences of naming navigation against a less tolerant Britain and a little of his journey to now.

Where I grew up

I grew up in London. I was born in Kensington, which is West London, the Royal Borough of Kensington and Chelsea. I call it a posh area because it's full of wealthy people who don't have to work for a living, but that wasn't true with my family. It just so happened that my father came to this country and landed in Kensington in a flat share, and then when he met my mother, she moved in, and over time, whoever was sharing the flat with him moved out as his family grew. So that's how I grew up in Kensington. Specifically, I was in the area known as High Street Kensington, and in that area, it was predominantly White. Still, if you went a bit further west, you hit Notting Hill Gate, a more diversely populated area with a much bigger Black community in Notting Hill.

Pronouncing my name

I've been to Armenia twice; the last time was in 1980 as a tourist when it was still part of the Soviet Union. I also recall going as a young kid and feeling like my name was just like any other.

In the UK, there is always a hesitancy. Generally speaking, people will say, "Aman". So, they don't roll the "R", and I've got to this. I mean the past, maybe 15 or 20 years of my life. I've got to a stage where I go with that. It's fine by me; "Aman" is fine. What occasionally bugs me is if people haven't heard it correctly the first time and don't ask me to repeat it. I don't mind repeating it, but what bugs me is if they don't ask me to repeat it and then will call me an approximation of what they think they've heard. Often, I'll get Armand with a "D" on the end or Ahmed, which is an entirely different name. When people call me Ahmed back, it's not just mishearing. It's them making some statement, I think. And the statement is, "Well, it sounded foreign, and I'm going to say this." And that I won't allow. That makes me furious when people call me Ahmed. It's also a very different name culturally. I'm not a religious person. I was brought up Orthodox Christian, but anyone with any nouse knows that Ahmed is a name from the Islamic culture. It's not a Christian name. I'm not anti-Islam at all, in any way, shape, or form, but culturally, it is a different name, so don't call me something that is not my name. So that bugs me a bit, but I will correct people. I don't let that slip, but I'm happy to go with Aman these days. And if they don't roll the "R", life has more complicated things to deal with.

For the most part, people are conscientious and want to correct it. So, when we were acting, and I introduced myself, I would see that moment behind people's eyes where they're processing, they think, "Did I quite hear that right?" but they don't repeat it. They don't say it back. Whereas I might have, I don't know, Peter or Sarah to my side, they'll say, "Hi, Sarah!" "Hi, Peter!" But with me, it's a "Hi!" "Hello!" Again, I noticed it in that instance, but I let it pass. It's still noticeable and reinforces a bit of being the outsider that there's still a difference.

Years ago, there used to be a programme called *This Is Your Life*, presented by an Irish guy called Eamonn Andrews. Essentially, they'll get a celebrity on. He'd surprise a celebrity, he'd carry a big red book, and they'd be out at some function, and he'd appear from nowhere, this guy, Eamonn Andrews, and surprise him and say this is your life, and you take them back to the studio, and for half an hour, he'd go through their life and bring guests along. Anyway, why am I going into detail about Eamonn Andrews? He was an Irish guy, but people thought somehow they heard Eamonn when I said Armen. That's a very different name because they were familiar with Eamonn.

I still have a friend whose dad calls me Armon. I don't put him right because I find it endearing for me. It makes me laugh because his son has repeatedly told him, "Dad, it's this." "All right, yeah. All right. So, Armon", that to me is endearing, so I just let that go. But if it were a stranger, I'd put them right because I find that annoying. It's not offensive as such, but I find it irritating.

There are still times when fleetingly I think, I wish I could say it, and it would be that easy, and the person will just pick it up straight away. Or I wish I could say it and not have to spell it out, so there are still those occasions when I think that. But given that life is so hard in so many more meaningful ways, it is what it is, but I still wish there weren't those times when I didn't have to spell it out or very consciously have to say it so that the other person gets it emphatically. And there are times when people make a judgement based on it. And there are times when people regard me as foreign simply because of my name, even though it's not openly expressed. But I can't change that. So, it is what it is.

I'm always pleasantly surprised if someone has said to me, "Well, I know a lot of Armen", or they pronounce it straight away the way it's correctly pronounced. That's always a pleasant surprise. And perhaps subconsciously, I do warm to them more. I'm more at ease with them quicker. But it's subconscious; it's not a conscious response on my part. I don't take against anyone who doesn't pronounce it Armen, but I do take against people who take it way offline.

I have one work colleague I don't work with often, but every time I work with him and his wife, they will consciously say "Armen". They will roll the "R" and sometimes overdo it to compass that Armen, which is fine. That feels good when people put that extra effort in, but I'm not in the least judgemental of those who don't put the extra effort in. As I say, it's okay.

They'll often ask me to repeat it, and that's okay. I'm not annoyed by that. Sometimes I am, but generally, I'm not. Yeah, if they ask me to repeat it, that's fine. There are instances where I'll repeat it, and still, I won't be referred to by name for the rest of that interaction because I know, I acknowledge, it's not a common name. It's an out-of-the-ordinary name. Thank goodness society has developed, and we're past the point where we used to get, "Oh! That's a strange name", or "Well, that's an unusual name", that used to be the response. I don't get that anymore, but I accept it's sort of out of the ordinary. I don't expect people to get it right the first time or hear it right the first time. If you ask me to repeat it, I hope you listen more attentively as I repeat it. After that, refer to me by name, but it doesn't happen. Whereas someone from a more enlightened background in that they've lived somewhere more cosmopolitan or have a wider circle of people they interact with will get the name immediately. Whether professional or not, they'll get the name immediately.

I do anglicise it myself from time to time. Let's say I'm making a booking over the phone, and they'll ask before for my name. I'll never say it. I always say I spell my first name for you, A-R-M-E-N, and I need to emphasise it more. But as I'm saying this now, I'm kicking myself that I've got into this habit of saying I'll spell my first name. I never say it. Why am I kicking myself? Why should I have to? It's a habit I've developed, and that's my way of not anglicising it. Sometimes, I do it to make life easier, just to fit in.

Another thing that still irritates me to this day. So, if I say, Armen, I get the response, "Oh, you mean like the end of the prayer?" And

I have to say, "No, it's not like the end of the prayer because it's spelt A-R-M-E-N." But then that's my fault. Because if I pronounce it Armen, then perhaps I am leading them up a path where they think it is like the end of the prayer, but that's been a lifelong hindrance. I get it less and less now, but that used to piss me off, like the end of the prayer. People would go, "So, what's your name, Arman?" They go "Amen." As a kid, you get upset, worked up, and frustrated.

In the past

I do feel that pressure to anglicise it because, again, I'm talking historically now. There were times when I felt like my name was a burden. I have three older sisters with English names: Mary, Angela, and Jennifer. Then it got to me, and my dad decided, "No, my son has to have an Armenian name." You see, I just anglicised that name. So, growing up with those three sisters with English names, it felt like, "Why was I given the difficult name? Why was I given the hard name? Why was I given the name that occasionally meant I was bullied?"

It's nowhere near as bad now as I'm going to go back, maybe 30 or 40 years ago, when there was a lot more ignorance about my country of origin. I have to go back generations, but it's Armenia, and there was a lot of ignorance about that 30 or 40 years ago. It's less now. What's the point I'm trying to make? The ignorance of 30 or 40 years ago meant people thought they could repeat your name in a quirky way or, from their perspective, what they thought was funny, and expected you to buy into their humour. Fortunately, that doesn't happen anymore, but I've also been through the mill with all that.

Throughout my childhood, I had to deal with so much, being called "armpit" and "almond". Almond, like the nut.

I can remember being picked on for many reasons at school, but one was because of my name. They'd often say, "You're an Arab then?", which is a sort of racism, again, born of ignorance. And having on one occasion, I'm talking about in my early teens, having a Union Jack thrust in my face by racist bullies at school, and part of that would have had to do with my name being different. You're an Arab, I hate the word, but I'll use it in this context, you are a Paki, but born of ignorance. But then highly offensive, hurtful, and distressing when you're 12 to 13. So, would I have wished I had a different name back then? Of course! Because then I wouldn't get picked on and have a Union Jack thrust in my face by racist bullies. But you go through it, and you come out the other end.

Growing up as a teenager was always a differentiator because you were regarded as foreign, and you would say, I was born here. Oh, yeah, but you're still foreign, aren't you? Again, that's growing up. So it went on as late as when I went to drama school back in the early 1990s, where it was expected there was no threat. It wasn't a massive drama school, so it was known throughout the school that I was born in London. I was in the UK, but one of the tutors turned to the rest of the class and said, "Oh, it's okay; he's foreign." I didn't challenge it at the time because, those days, you didn't challenge things like that.

So, growing up and as a teenager, it always felt like a label. You're the foreigner. I can remember saying I was born in Kensington in an over-posh way as a means of fitting. At school, there were no other Armen, so I got bullied and teased. I suggest teasing more. Kids like to find something to make fun of people because kids are kids.

Only when I got to a university did it become less of a factor because I went around with a group of my peers, and quite a few had foreign names. So, it was okay. But yeah, there were times when you went out socially and introduced yourself to someone, which still felt awkward. I've got to say my name, or they'll judge me based on it. He's a foreign-type thing, which is not relevant now but was back then. Nowadays, people wouldn't do it because they're more sensitive, conscientious, etc., but they were offensive back then.

Now, one might get picked on differently. It's many years since I've, I don't know, I'm making a presumption. It's many years since I've formally applied for a job. It's all done through computers, but if you get through the computer around to a human being seeing your application form. And if they see the name Armen, does that still inform their perception of this candidate? Quite possibly.

And now

I've been to New York countless times over the years. At least four times, I've been pulled over, whether because of the name on my passport or because I had a beard while travelling. Who knows? It could be one or the other, or it could be neither. I've been travelling with other people with English names and have just been let through with them.

Now, there needs to be more knowledge and awareness of the name. Again, it's not explicitly said, but I still pick up the reactions in trying to place me as my surname is Gregory, which is anglicised (not by me, but generations back). People are trying to figure out how the two names go together. You know, how does one go with the other? That's so foreign, and that isn't. So, I'll be asked occasionally why your first name is foreign. And then I have to explain. I try to briefly explain that going back at least two or three generations, my surname was anglicised as I've been told to make it easier for English people to pronounce it.

It's worth mentioning that my actual surname is Gregorian. Generally speaking, all Armenian surnames will end in I-A-N. And it was a chant, a Gregorian chant, but not connected to the Gregorian chants. And then, at least three generations ago, my great-grandparents and all Armenians living within the British Empire were encouraged to anglicise their surnames to make it easier for the English to pronounce them. So, that's how I have the surname Gregory instead of Gregorian. It's a blessing not to have the name Armen Gregorian. It would have made life even harder, especially when going for (acting) auditions.

Acting life

One looks the way one looks, and we know from experience that you are cast often based on the look. But the name Armen didn't fit in with how a foreigner – in inverted commas – might speak. The look was that you're always going to cast as non-English, but the name was also added to it. In 1982, Ben Kingsley came to prominence playing Gandhi. And the look of Ben Kingsley was undoubtedly not someone English, and he was playing the most well-known person of Asian Indian origin. So, I remember thinking, well, he's called Ben Kingsley, but he doesn't look like a Ben. He looks foreign. I could stand a chance, even with a name like Armen, in playing English roles because Ben Kingsley went on to play several English roles. As we know now, he has played several different nationalities. Why did I get into that? Because you aspire to be like people who made it or are making it. So that's why I got into that. So, I thought there was some hope with a name like Armen.

So, how do I say my name and make it sound anglicised? At the same time, I know I'm being seen for an English role. Painful. Foolishly, for a short while, I changed my professional name to Mac, M-A-C, because my uncle, my father's brother, was called Mac. And I respected and admired him. He was a poet. He used to sell his poems on South Beach in Miami. And I respected him because somehow, he was this romantic figure, selling books of poems on South Beach. He hardly earned a penny.

I changed my name to Mac Gregory because I thought it would make life easier, and I'd be seen for more roles, and people would only see me as foreign because I had a foreign first name. It was ridiculous because then people were curious if I was Scottish, given the name Mac Gregory. I'd have to say, "No, I'm not", and then go into a whole explanation. Anyway, it lasted about two years, before I reverted to Armen.

Sometimes, I have to go to networking events. I dislike them. I wouldn't say I like networking events because they're so artificial, and I know you need to embrace them for what they are, but I've never liked those events where I'm talking to you, but I'm looking over your shoulder to see who I can go and talk to next. I only rarely raise the subject because, in one sense, having a name badge with my name on it meant lack of pressure because it means that my name is there, that people can look at it, and I don't have to say it. They could look at it, and if they choose to speak to me by name, having looked at it first, all well and good, and sometimes they might ask me, "How do you pronounce your first name?" All is well and good. And in the third instance, if they see it and still don't refer to me by name, all is well and good. But that's just prompted me to think about that. That was the last networking event I went to; maybe that was six months ago. I held onto the name badge. It's in my bag somewhere. I've always got it there. Why do I have it? That may be the future, that I will always have a name badge about my person. So, in ten years, if I can't be bothered to say my name, I hold the badge up. There you go.

Importance of names

Let's call people by the name they were given correctly. We refer to people by the name that they were given and pronounce it correctly because, to me, that is respect. It's about respect. It's being respectful to them. I've made an effort, but it's about something other than making an effort. I will always consciously attempt to clarify how someone's name is pronounced if it's a name that is new to me. I want to get it right out of respect for them. And if they say to me, "But you can just say this", I will always say, "But please let me try to say your name how it should be pronounced", because that's respectful.

So, whether they be new students or people I meet through work, if they say their name, I have yet to hear it correctly. I will say, "Do you mind repeating your name?" And they do, and then, I need to pronounce their name the way it should be. For instance, on a recent course I teach, we've had overseas students from the Far East whose names are complex in terms of their pronunciation, and some have chosen to anglicise them for ease's sake, and some have not. I'm not saying one is exemplary or the other. For those who don't choose to anglicise their name, I will consciously attempt to pronounce it the way it should be noted because it's respectful to them.

Another teaching example: a few years ago, a Polish student was on a course, and his surname ended with a "shh" sound. But everyone kept saying the S as ending in s, so I would always refer to him as "shh" and end with an "S". It's their choice. He didn't choose to get them to pronounce it the way he did, but whatever it is now, it's still easier than it was years ago, so much easier as the world has gotten smaller in terms of ease of travel. It has become more accessible, but I'm talking about big-city life. If I lived in some remote village in the Scottish Highlands, I'd still be encountering daily mispronunciations that would get my back up. But living in London has been a lot better. So fundamentally, it boils down to respect for each other. Yeah, I respect you enough. That's the wrong word. I appreciate you, so I will say how your name should be pronounced. It's a simple thing. It doesn't cost anything.

I respect the person trying. I appreciate them for attempting to respect me by getting the name right or pronouncing it right. That's not to say I disrespect those who don't, but I outwardly or inwardly smile if someone's trying to pronounce it the way it should be because I think good of you. There are no fair dues. You're making that attempt. It costs nothing. It costs another 10 seconds of thought and 20 seconds to say it the right way. Otherwise, it's idleness. It's being lazy.

If things keep improving, down to people like you who are conscientious in doing these projects because you're doing it on your own, no one's told you to; you're to be respected and admired for that. I mean that sincerely. But that's the only way we're also going to perpetuate change.

Changes to the Whiteness ecology over time

Armen's story represents that while the challenges may have changed, and name bias may have lessened over time, Whiteness ecology remains a consistent backdrop. While adverse reactions to his name were much more hostile in their prejudice in the past, his recent experiences indicate a subtle yet still problematic name navigation dynamic. Armen's experiences allude to much of what Dheeraj references when comparing his experiences with his parents' generation.

As has become a running theme across all the stories so far, Armen recounts attempts to assimilate or being under pressure to assimilate by altering his name. Interestingly, Armen perceives a positive social shift in name acceptance, though he does reference recent experiences where he still encounters challenges to people correctly pronouncing his name. From a Whiteness ecology perspective, it can be concluded that markers of assimilation, socialisation into so-called British norms, and overt racism in the shape of past right-wing groups such as the National Front, for example, have changed – they have merely been replaced with more subtle markers that continue to place pressure on individuals to compromise on their name identity for the comfort of others.

Armen and Javeria share similar experiences in the context of their diasporas and wanting to "fit in". Both allude to an early need to be seen and accepted as British, and their stories represent how they grappled with issues of belonging from a young age. Learning that we can take away from this is to consider the impact our interactions have on others, particularly young people, on first introductions where they may be sharing a name, we are unfamiliar with. How might we make them feel safe and comfortable? What strategies might we adopt to ensure that we engage sensitively and respectfully and learn the correct pronunciation of names?

7
My name is Syra

Understanding mixed heritage name navigation

- To assist readers in making connections between broader social and identity contexts and name navigation.
- To provide readers with an insight into how name navigation can be an ongoing process for some based on their past and present experiences.
- Readers are given the opportunity to draw from the Whiteness ecology theory application that the author has modelled in previous chapters to attempt their own application to this story.

Background

Yeah. Okay, so my name, right? I'll go back really to an early point. So, I come from a mixed heritage family. My dad is Pakistani, and my mum is from a White Irish background. My mum always told me she wanted to call me Sophia, interestingly. But my dad was keen on Saera. So, they settled on Saera.

Pronunciation

Now, the original spelling of my name is different from how my name was spelt. So my original spelling is S-A-E-R-A, but unfortunately, what I found over my entire childhood and earlier adult life was that people could only pronounce it as Saera when they read it. Some people don't have an E, and they have an I instead. So, about 28 years ago, I decided to change the spelling to S-Y-R-A as it is now.

There wasn't anything significant or any particular event that made me change the spelling. I graduated from my undergraduate degree programme and then took up my first graduate-level role. And I was pretty conscious that I'd be mixing with many people who might struggle with my name professionally. So I'm trying to minimise some of that disruption and some of that unnecessary distraction or whatever you want to call it. By then changing the spelling, my undergraduate degree was actually in a foreign language, and I had many problems with my name pronunciation during that time because a lot of people on my course were people from the global majority and I also spent one year of the degree programme living abroad as well in North Africa. So, it only bothered me a little during those four years of my undergraduate degree. But yeah, going into a graduate level role was probably the turning point of why I thought I ought to, alter the spelling just slightly to make it easier for people to pronounce.

Often, I don't even get called my first name. I get called my surname in emails, which I find strange. It's difficult to understand why this happens, but I think it may be because people don't take the time to look at my name and ask me about its pronunciation. There have been instances in meetings where my name has been mispronounced repeatedly, and although I have corrected the person on every occasion, I have become frustrated. However, I haven't expressed my frustration openly, and this has made others uncomfortable. There have been times when people have asked me why my name is being pronounced incorrectly, and this has resulted in a loss of productivity.

In the past

I do remember, as a child, dreading the school register experiences in the classroom, mainly if there was a cover teacher or a cover supervisor in the post. I used to get anxious and anticipate when it came to my name in the register. Eventually, I started to feel a little bit more confident that before they even got to my name, I'd kind of stop the teacher and say, my name is, and then tell them my name to avoid that horrible embarrassment and all the other children laughing in my face in the classroom. I did go to a predominantly white school, so I was conscious of the fact that I was brown and my name was very, very different from the other children in the classroom.

Making an effort to get a name right

So I am increasingly conscious that it affects many people around you when someone repeatedly mispronounces your name. So there is that solidarity to some extent that other people recognise just how important it is to get people's names right and how it can negatively impact their experience. For me, names are so important for people's identity and that you try to get someone's name right. I mispronounce people's names sometimes, and

I have a suspicion that I might've got it wrong, so I'll check in with that person to make sure I've got it right and then maybe read it over and over in my head to make sure I'm going to get it right on the subsequent occasion.

But we must make an effort with that. In recent years, there has been growing awareness about getting people's gender pronouns correct. Unfortunately, a similar emphasis isn't placed on getting people's names right. For me, the name is a primary part of somebody's identity. That's how you're referred to. That's how you're called. That's how you are spoken to. It's usually one of the main things that people introduce themselves with when they first meet someone before they even talk about their gender identity or other aspects of who they are. So, for me, getting someone's name correct or trying to learn someone's name and say it correctly is significant and should be first area of focus.

So that's been something that I've reflected on more recently. Names can connect to people's heritage and background, their parents, their family, where they come from, the geographical location where they were born, perhaps, or where their family was born. It may also have something to do with how people have moved around the world. So, there's so much more than just the name. It's a reflection of people's identity and who they are. People might have changed their names, and there might be some actual purposes behind that, too, a whole story and an entire narrative we don't know. So the importance of somebody's name. It shouldn't be underestimated and should be thought about at a deeper level.

My relationship with my name (changes over time)

It could be as you get older and feel more and more comfortable in your skin, you feel more and more comfortable in your identity and who you are, and maybe my geographical movement has something to do with that. When I turned 18 to attend university for my undergraduate degree, I moved to an ethnically diverse city. The same happened when I moved, did my master's degree programme, and stayed. I never returned to where my family lived, a predominantly white-populated city in the north-east. So, I became more comfortable with who I am and my background.

And so comes that acceptance of my name, my diversity, who I am, and that sort of thing. But because my professional background has been in social work, there's a lot of reflective practice that one does as a practitioner. And then as I've got older, I use other mediums of reflective practice, whether that's when I go running or exercising or whatever, or at the end of the day when I'm sitting down and thinking about what I've done and what I'm going to be doing tomorrow, I guess then that these periods of reflection allow you to take care of yourself, that sort of self-care and have that kind of happiness in who you are, irrespective of faults and everything else. So, yeah. So maybe there's been a combination of different things that have led to this point.

- How would you apply Whiteness ecology theory to Syra's story?
- Can you identify representations of the micro, maeso, and macro systems in Syra's story?

- Based on Whiteness ecology, how does Whiteness play out in Syra's experiences of name navigation? Can you identify any prevalent themes?
- What have you learnt from Syra's story?
- How do you aim to implement any learning into your inter-actions or practice after reading Syra's story?

8
My name is Phoenix

Understanding the challenges of name navigation in the context of experience and embodiment

- To assist readers in making connections between broader identity contexts and name navigation.
- To provide readers with an insight into how name navigation can be an ongoing process.
- Readers can draw from the Whiteness ecology theory application that the author has modelled in previous chapters to attempt their application to this story.

About me

So I was born Kay, K-A-Y, and my name has always been very simple, very plain. The uniqueness of my name, Nacto, comes from my father's last name, which is from the island of Guadeloupe. When I was born, my mother's last name was a derivative of the island of Saint Kitts and Nevis, a very British name, and then, of course, a very francophone name. I've had both.

My background

So, growing up, my first name was Kay Nadine. It's Kay; my middle name is Nadine. My name Kay comes from my father's name, which is Clé, which in French means essential, and my dad always said that my name was the key to opening up any door of possibility or the key to his heart.

As I grew up, though, most of my family called me by my middle name, Nadine. So, it was screamed around the house; that was what I was called. That's what my sister called me, my aunts, and everyone else. Nacto is always very difficult for people to pronounce, so I've heard a lot of versions of it growing up. It was always bizarre, and I always felt proud of that. I felt unique about that with my last name, because my first name is so plain.

And I kept my middle name at home; you don't know my middle name unless you're in my family. So as I got older, as everyone else does, when you have an identity crisis, you're just thinking of names; I want to be called something else. I didn't choose this name.

Impact of my art on my name identity

I started to do spoken word, and Kay could have sounded more fun. It didn't reflect the intense darkness that was my angst, my teen angst. It didn't fit my teen angst, so I started with Black but spelled B-L-A-Q-U-E uniquely. This story is going to be interesting. So I went by Blaque, and that's how everyone knew me, especially in a spoken word society; it was my nickname.

So that lasted up until University. When I got to university, I started to get into my groove with poetry and expressing myself artistically. As I grew, I was performing more. It's been a decade since my new name has evolved, and it came out of a professor or somebody who saw me perform, but they told me I have such a fire about myself.

They were like, man, Blaque is such a dark name, and I never saw it dark or sad. It embodied my poetry at the time, but Blaque is beautiful; Blaque has so many different connotations to it, and of course, I was attending a historically black college in the United States at the time. So it was fantastic.

I can't remember if it was a professor or someone who saw me perform, but they said, "There's such fire about the way that you present or talk; there's always this flame around you." And I was sitting there, thinking and wrestling with this name that I had, and everyone was getting to know me by, and I was, of course, going through a little bit of another identity crisis.

So that's how Phoenix came up, and ever since I started to use that name, as I tell more of my story, it makes sense to me. Phoenix grew on me, and when I researched what it was and what it meant, I was just like, yep, because the moment that it was happening, this kind of growth that occurs in university time, I was growing out of that darkness, and I was finding myself.

There, I was becoming more of me. This is the second time in my life that I have reinvented myself. So, it shows this kind of death and rebirth that I tend to do, which goes with many of my experiences throughout my life. Because of this death and resurrection, and not being afraid of starting over and doing something new, the Phoenix made sense because I tend to be reborn. I'm not scared of death.

Being Phoenix

So Phoenix just came up and left the stage; it went to my work. So whenever I saw it, wrote my essays, or started handing in my essays that way, my professors began to get to know me as that. Then, instead of seeing Kay on campus, they saw Phoenix on campus. So, my name just started to follow me, and I decided to do my master's in the UK.

It felt so poetic, but when my professor wrote my letter of recommendation, she wrote it as Phoenix. So, of course, there's always been the struggle over the past ten years of my life, where my passport or ID card says Kay, but everyone calls me Phoenix. So sometimes when I have to write official documentation, they're like, "Who's this person?", because "We know you were Phoenix."

I remember one of my friends being shocked years later; as I started doing my PhD, they were just like, "So your name is Kay", and I was like, "Unfortunately, yes". Because everyone knows me as Phoenix. So, I used to put my name, Phoenix, in brackets and my last name. So, when I started to do my PhD, I saw a professor, and he was like, "What is the brackets thing? Are you Phoenix?" "Yes." "Well, get the brackets out of that, be Phoenix. You know what, contact HR and see if you could put your name." I am grateful to the LGBTQ community, and this naming of yourself with your identity and sexuality, that I was able to do.

Navigating the two-name identities

Yes, there are the official documents that have to go out, but for the most part, as a lecturer, my official title with my email address and everything is Phoenix. Those who know, they know, but for the most part, I'm Phoenix to everyone. It's so great, it's so funny because I had a colleague named Kay, as well. Imagine the confusion that would have happened had there been two Kays in the department.

But I have been so lucky that what started as a stage name has become something I identify with.

My father and I didn't see eye to eye, but more specifically, my father and I have his birthday; my first name came from his name. We are similar in many ways, but we had such a history with each other that I wanted something so far away from him. For a long time, I was going to get rid of my family's last name because I always felt like the black sheep, and being this black sheep, I didn't feel I suited Kay or Nacto. I didn't fit in.

It's been longer than five years. It was during college, and as I started to get known beyond poetry nights as Phoenix, I was like, "Well, why don't I change everything?" So, I remember one night, I think I was in my mid-20s. I was like, "My goodness! Where am I?" So if I'm not this or that, I'm somewhere in the middle, so that means a little bit of a grey, but if I'm going to be Phoenix Grey, I don't want to spell it G-R-A-Y or the colour G-R-E-Y.

I sat down, and I was like, "How do I want to spell it?" if this is going to be my last name. If people knew me like this and thought about my PhD, I would be docked at Phoenix Grey. Doesn't that sound nice? How do I want to get known? And so I spelt it G-R-E-I-G-H, like Ashleigh, that long spelling of that. I had this in my heart for such a long time.

Now, be it that my father and I are so removed from each other, it's been a while since we've been around each other. And so when he came to the UK and met people who knew me, many people were saying Phoenix. My mum got used to it. Before she used to say, "Who's Phoenix?", but she knew over the past ten years of this gradual, and specifically the last five years, that everyone in my cohort, my co-workers, my students know me as that, so she's gotten used to it. But my dad, on the other hand, it was such an exciting experience to see him like, "Well, I mean, if this is who you are."

And there was a level of acceptance and a lot of healing. That's what happened. I don't know how much time we have left, but I think one of the things that has kept my name so relevant to my life is the last six months, actually of the previous five years, I would say four years, and then the pandemic, but six months specifically, I was having a rough time with my PhD. And I was between a rock and a hard place.

I know this cycle, but for whatever reason, the death is not happening. I feel like I want to be reborn. I feel like there is a new start for me, but for whatever reason, the flame isn't burning for the death and rebirth to happen. And my therapist said to me, "Well, what if what you're going through is drowning you in water rather than flaming you with fire? I said, 'Oh!'"

When they said that to me, they said you're used to this fire; you know how to handle it, and that sparks you. And if you're in something that does not light you up and instead drowns you out, that might be a signal to something because you felt like you were drowning, and, that doesn't work for who you are.

It was a lightbulb moment, so it gave me clarity about myself and my situation and my decision not to continue with my PhD, well, for now. So now, to pause my PhD, to take myself out of higher education forum for a bit to look at it differently because I'm very artistic. I don't know if my artistic desires fit in a particular mode, and I don't know how to get out of it for now.

So I need a new view, but that conversation, and I don't know where you would put that or how you would put that as you write it out, but I think that that was something that brought it full circle for me, with Phoenix and how it's not just a name. It has followed me over the past decade, being part of these critical moments of my life.

Before I finish this PhD, I need to be able to put Phoenix Greigh on everything officially. I want to hear that name called out when they want to hand in my diploma. So that means I have to return to the United States and do that process. I still need to do it because you might have a plan, but the universe has its own thing. Again, I am trying to figure out things about myself. Is this what I want? And I couldn't put my finger on it. I'm okay with sharing this, and if this will help someone. So I went to therapy, and I was explaining my name. Even if I get to the lowest of lows, that means the death is happening, that means I am reborn, I start over.

Married life and exposure to others' cultural name navigations

I met my husband, Traore, and he's a beautiful Senegalese man with a lovely family. And in falling in love with him and this family, much of the trauma healed. And I'm not saying that I've gotten rid of the idea of changing my last name to Greigh or hyphenating it with Traore, which is my husband's last name, but I found that I didn't have that contention with the last name that I was born with, such as the previous name for my father.

Something funny. I don't know where you put it, but very rarely does my husband, who knows my first name, very rarely does my husband say Kay. So he says, my wife, partner, my love, or Phoenix. So, whenever he says my name, I'm like, "Who, what?" And it's so interesting because he understands my name and its importance to me.

So, if he sees that I'm not being myself and he's like, "Remember your name." And that's one of those things where it's been beyond something. I've had such a transition. This kind of evolution continues to happen. So what started as Kay Nadine Nacto may end up as Phoenix Greigh Traore on all my documents. Cross fingers. It just takes such a long time because you have to put in the newspaper for 180 days and go in front of a judge and I don't have time to go to the States.

Affirming Phoenix

It is something that will happen before my 40th birthday. It's about something other than what needs to be on the certificate for my PhD. If it's never on anything official, if all my friends and the people who know me and understand me know me by Phoenix, that's good enough. It's no longer I have to have it official; it's nice. It is very nice when I see a document, especially at work; those are great moments.

Maybe that is something I will work towards. Okay. 40th is a little far, for now, 35. I have a couple of years for that one. If I could do it before 35, that would be a great birthday gift. But if I can transition between those two people and two names because of the journey, that would be wonderful. I hope that's me.

- How would you apply Whiteness ecology theory to Phoenix's story?
- Can you identify representations of the micro, maeso, and macro systems in Phoenix's story?
- Based on Whiteness ecology, how does Whiteness play out in Phoenix's experiences of name navigation? Can you identify any prevalent themes?
- What have you learnt from Phoenix's story?
- How do you aim to implement any learning into your interactions or practice after reading Phoenix's story?

9
My name is Teeroumanee

Understanding name identity in the context of religion and ethnicity.

- To assist readers in making connections between religious, racial, and cultural significance to name navigation.
- Readers can draw from the Whiteness ecology theory application that the author has modelled in previous chapters to attempt their application to this story.

So, to start, my name is Teeroumanee, and I've also got a pet name at home that my family calls me. I've also got another pet name closer, dearer family and friends call me. So, the story around my name, so my name itself means sacred bells. So, if you consider, for example, holy bells in temples and churches, they're also significantly related to music, as is my last name, which is primarily related to music. I thought I did not know the meaning of my name growing up until I was probably about ten because the name is a South Indian name, and I come from Mauritius. We speak Creole here.

Racial and cultural background

We don't speak South Indian languages as much in our house-holds. So it was only when I was teaching Asian languages in primary school that I came to know, oh, by the way, this is what my name is, and later on, I came to know that my name is also mentioned in some prayers, something like that. However, I connect with my name, there is a particular sort of vibrancy there, for example, I do a lot of meditation. People familiar with meditation and things like that will probably know the gong sound when you hear it, and then you refocus, bringing back your awareness.

No, I can't say that I've always been like this, but I've learnt to be. And then it's only later that I realised that this is what my name is telling me exactly, and this is the type of path that I'm taking because I'm more spiritual than religious now. After all, travelling has opened me up to more religions, ethnicities, and cultures. It made me more spiritual than religious, and I believe Teeroumanee has meant a lot over the last 15 years. My first step outside of my country was about 18 years or 19 years ago, and I think that's when my name started to mean more to me because growing up, my parents, were calling me by my pet name rather than my official name.

Racial and cultural ramifications to name pronunciation

So it's only outside the country that people start calling me by my official name, by my official first name. In the UK, it's been a diffi-cult journey regarding my name. I've had all sorts of abbreviations.

I think it's typically British to sometimes abbreviating names there, which I don't like. Some have happened without my permission, so people feel it's alright to reduce my name to a T. I've had people call me Tee, just as in T-E-E, the first three alphabets of my first name. I've had some people who've called and written in emails, just capital T. I wonder how lazy that was. That wasn't very pleasant.

I've had someone who introduced me as "like it's not coffee; it's the other drink". So, I was T-E-A now. Tea as in the drink. This wasn't very pleasant because that person repeated it several times at work, in the office, and even when we would meet outside. He was like oh, do you know this is my colleague? By the way, her name is … It was upsetting, especially coming from a person of colour, and it is still upsetting when white people also make fun of my name or think that it's alright for them to spell it or write it however they want.

I've got loads of vowels in my name. I'm not specific if they miss an E or an A or put the E before the whatever, the alphabet wrongly, like once or twice if they do it; that's where I'm not going to pick on that, and I am aware that there's a lot … I've worked in the disability field before. So, I'm aware that there are people who have dyslexia. Some people have lots of other issues that they may not have diagnosed dyslexia to me, but they may find it difficult. So, I'm not very specific about those spelling, if they're writing. However, I do get a bit annoyed if they mispronounce it.

It's got to do with the sound. As I said, my name is very much linked to sound. So, because of that, I'm like, no, this is not my name, and anyway, when I was born, for us, names have a lot of meaning. So, you don't just put on a name to a kid; you check the date that the kid was born, the times and everything, and the stars and all sorts of things, and then you choose the alphabet that goes with a person. So you have two or three options, then select that one alphabet.

Obviously, the parents have got to pick one, then they choose one, and then they look for a name taught by that. So, it is a name that starts with a pronunciation and a sound that relates to me and my character. So, I do get very annoyed when people mispronounce it. I think before, I was not that annoyed, but the more I think that I've been in the UK and the more that I find people taking the liberty, taking the freedom to, just change my name without my consent. Would you suddenly just change the name of the queen who passed away or of the king? Not necessarily. You'll still respect them and use all the honours in front, king, queen, so why can't you say my name?

Understanding slavery and labour from an outside UK perspective has been very important in my understanding of colonialism. I keep asking myself, well, when they invaded the land of my ancestors, did the name of the people not bother them? Why can't they pronounce my name? They were saying all sorts of long names before. Yes, they did anglicise specific names. We find this in all the ex-British colonies, but yeah, for me, it's getting more and more annoying, getting my name just twisted and distorted, especially when people are talking to me.

And then you've got people who do make the effort. They'll, listen to how I pronounce my name. People who just hear my name, and they just repeat it a few times. They'll get it, but some people don't make the effort. You might have worked with them so often, and they don't make the effort. That is, if not annoying, it's frustrating and upsetting, and if it happens in a professional setting, it's very unprofessional. It's not collegial at all and unethical and, of course, racist. Let's not say we have to say it's racist. That's how it is; however, I don't take it upon myself to go and correct people.

I shouldn't be doing this because of the number of times that I've taken the time and effort to correct people. I'm just tired of that. It can also be gendered, for example, a woman called Chris, they'll think it's a man. We've got these biases. So, I've often got people reverse my official first and last names, but I've stopped correcting people. I'm just calling out on them publicly, and that's your publicity.

I would not be signing as T, Tee, or short-form emails. So I think I don't need to give them more chances, especially if it's in a professional setting because, for example, people who work in education or in organisations where there is DI [diversity and inclusion] training, all these are part of training, so, I shouldn't have to tell them what they're doing wrong. I call it out, and publicly, it will happen. It takes a lot of bravery to do that. Still, I think I'm at a stage where I cannot be bothered about protecting people who are racist or who take the liberty of just assuming that they can do whatever they want, especially if they are line managers and with senior positions that they can tweak things to their likings. That's a quick history.

This is where I am at the moment. I think I have been too fearful to call it out before, and also people of colour, whenever they face things around racism but it isn't always to do with racism. You've also got English names that are constantly shortened. If you are in a junior role or you're still navigating the UK workplace and stuff like this, you are still testing what's right and wrong. Are you still seeing the culture? Is that right? Then, you come across somebody else who has no problem saying your name right and respecting you. And then you figure out that, oh yes, it was just that person there, it was just this one person or just this set of people, group of people, and then now I'm just calling it out publicly, and that's where I stand at the moment, and I'm comfortable with my name. If somebody has a problem with it, that's their problem. I cannot be bothered. It's literally like physical appearance. If somebody has an issue with your physical appearance, it's their problem.

And I think it's a bit like body shaming. This one is name-shaming. We have to call it what it is, I believe, in the twenty-first century when we are talking more and more about racism openly. When we are talking more and more about inclusion, and when, fortunately, Black Lives Matter has revived in some way, unfortunately, I think it's time to change. It's time to make the change happen. We cannot just keep letting things like this go because a person's name has so much to do with their identity. It's a bit like you are a homeless person who can't have a bank account because they don't have an address. It's like a chicken and egg thing.

My relationship with my name

So, a name is equally as crucial as an address. It's all about stability and respect as well around your name. I take a stand on that, and if people are telling me that they are doing decolonisation work, anti-racism work, and inclusion work, whether it is amplifying inclusion for disability or other protected groups, then this should be a primary focus, calling someone by their name as it is.

Whether it's someone who's gay, someone who's disabled, whatever work you're doing around inclusion and DI. Getting the name of a person right is essential, right? Because you can't be conversing with someone, if they are continuously not pronouncing my name right even after they've heard my name a hundred times, that's not a conversation because I'll switch off. Something that happened earlier this year, I attended a meeting about belongingness. It was online. I signed in on the platform, Teeroumanee, my full name, as in my full first name, and the person called me Tee. I switched off the whole meeting; I switched off for an entire hour.

I couldn't be bothered. I could have contributed. I couldn't be bothered. I didn't contribute to any activity because there's no point in me doing anything when you are talking about belongingness and being disrespectful towards me. So I take a stand on that. As I said, if someone has, for the first time, made a mistake in pronouncing my name or a couple of times made a typo in an email, that doesn't bother me that much. Still, if it's consistently done, it tells you, oh, names don't matter. Racism exists, it's like that, exactly like that.

- How would you apply Whiteness ecology theory to Teeroumanee's story?
- Can you identify representations of the micro, maeso, and macro systems in Teeroumanee's story?
- Based on Whiteness ecology, how does Whiteness play out in Teeroumanee's experiences of name navigation? Can you identify any prevalent themes?
- What have you learnt from Teeroumanee's story?
- How do you aim to implement any learning into your interactions or practice after reading Teeroumanee's story?

10
My name is Georgina

Understanding the significance of name identity in the context of mixed heritage and post-colonial connections

- Readers will consider the nuances of name navigation in the context of mixed heritage post-colonial identities.
- Readers can draw from the Whiteness ecology theory application that the author has modelled in previous chapters to attempt their application to this story.

My name and its origins

So I have a very long name. My full name is Hlamalani Georgina Kraft Makhubele. The name is very loaded in the sense that I am South African. My dad is black, and my mum is white. So the associations of that in terms of our country's history are pretty hectic. And so, Hlamalani was given to me by my dad. He is Tonga or Shanghan. And it was a name I went by when I was small, but I can't remember exactly when; I think I was like four. I decided I didn't want to go by that anymore. And to put that into context, I didn't grow up with my dad. I grew up with my mum and so grew up in White spaces. And even as a young child, I would get frustrated with people mispronouncing my name. Subconsciously, I wanted to assimilate. So even though South Africa is primarily black and of colour, I was in a very White space. I thought I had named myself Georgina, but I don't know why. I remember saying, "Today, I'm Georgina", and that's it. Obviously, I was convinced I gave myself this name when I didn't. I got it from my mum. Her dad was Afrikaans, and her mum was British. I was named after a great-grandfather, George, and another family member, Georgina. Then Kraft is obviously from my mum, a very Afrikaans surname. And then Makhubele is my dad.

So there's just a lot there. And growing up, once I had decided, "Cool, I'm Georgina", I always went by Georgina Kraft until I reached high school. Because my surname wasn't officially Kraft, it was Makhubele; I had to switch. And that was quite strange because everyone didn't know me like that. And I still have friends from that context who would refer to me as Kraft, not Makhubele. There's so much to sort through, but over time and as I've gotten older, I've felt like I've wanted to claim my first name as my first name. I still feel anxious about introducing myself as Hlamalani or Georgina.

I went by Georgina for my entire childhood except when I was tiny. Then, university friends would use it more because that's also when I stepped away from my bubble, and I was sur-rounded by many different types of people, including people who celebrated that I was Hlamalani and Georgina. And they were like, "Oh my gosh." "That's your name?" "That's so cool." It only started from my undergrad in South Africa. And then, obviously, my dad calls me Hlamalani, and people on my dad's side of the family.

To add more confusion, I started making music and a big thing with that was, what would my name be? And I was thinking of using Hlamalani, but then on a larger scale, South Africa is excellent, but the rest of the world is confused. However, I had a flatmate who was Welsh, and she could say it perfectly. But because the Welsh have the same sounds, I was like, "This is crazy." But deciding what I wanted my name to be in that context was also a whole process. And I ended up going with a name that reflected both sides. So it's Venus Vulhani and Vulhani is also Shanghan. And I wanted to keep both parts of me in there because it felt like if I just used an English name, it wouldn't feel authentic to who I am, even though it's a character it's still me.

Moving to the UK

Moving to the UK depends on the context, right? So I only have a few friends and family members who even refer to me as Hlamalani. It's weird how to change the people's minds you've grown up with. Like, "Oh, please, can you call me this?" But also because I feel attached to both. So it's an exciting line to walk. But weirdly, after I studied at Central and did a music diploma, they needed a section for preferred names there. So, what is your name, and what would you like to be called? And officially, I'm Hlamalani.

And so, it was extraordinary to be in a British context where there were all of these teachers and students around me, none of them South African or even African, calling me Hlamalani. And I was like, "Okay, cool, this is strange." I haven't had this before. I try to remember people constantly referring to me by my first name. But with that also, a thing mentioned in the documentary, the classic reading of an attendance register. And you know they've gotten to your name, and they're like, "Sorry, I know I'm going to say it wrong." And then you're like, "No, it's fine." And then they're like, "Give it a go." And you're like, "Hlamalani." And they're like, "Hello, Malani." And you're like, "Hlamalani." And then you're just like, "Yeah, okay." "Cool, that's fine." It's just too much because of the emotional energy and effort to try and get someone to say your name correctly. And you can tell they're trying, but they're never really going to get there because it's like a sound that isn't normal in English. Eventually, I would always say, "It's fine; you can call me Georgina or George." And they're like, "What, where does that come from?" And I'm like, "I haven't just made it up; it's also my second name."

So there are so many parts to. It feels like it's never just a simple, this, is it? Because even when I'm writing an email or applying for a job, I'm like, do I use my full name or a name that feels less intimidating to make it easier? And you wonder, does that affect someone's perception of you because it's like a foreign name? And something interesting that came up in my thoughts while watching the documentary – well, not interesting – something I experienced was that at the graduation at Central, you have to put in your name and the phonetic spelling of that name and for Hlamalani, there's no English phonetic spelling for it. So I remember saying, "I don't know how I'm going to do this." This is a disaster waiting to happen. And weirdly, it was alright. They had talked to someone. I don't know who they would've spoken to, but it wasn't a disaster. But it was just the anxiety before, there's no way for me to write this in English.

When returning to South Africa

Of course, in terms of context, it goes further because even in a South African context, my favourite is when I arrive back at Border Control in Cape Town, and the border police always look at my passport, and they are so confused. They expect a darker person to be in front of them, who looks more typical of Hlamalani, right? And so, I'm there with my straight hair with an in-between accent, and they're like, "What?" So I'm asked, "Are you married to an African man?" I get confused looks. I find it entertaining. I don't find it offensive at all. I'm like, "Yeah, strange." But it's always a question mark when I come back to South Africa. So it's a weird in-betweenness that I think I've always experienced with being a mixed-race person in South Africa. There are just so many connotations beyond the name.

Identifying with my name

I don't go by Hlamalani often, but I feel more whole when I am called it. It feels like it makes sense. But I go by Georgina so often that that's just my default. And so, that's just me in my head.

It was like two things. It was like, cool. It is possible to say less, and people will get by. But at the same time, they will get it primarily wrong, at least initially, and it will be frustrating. And I will want to go, "No, it's fine." "It's okay, call me Georgina, it's easier." Yeah, it did affirm that it would be hard work, but it could also work out.

It is still a process. And after watching that documentary, I was like, I should ask the people around me. I had a friend who said, "Yeah, another friend of ours and I call you Tummy, which is like a shorter version of Hlamalani." And it made me so happy, and

I was like, "Oh my God." "Really, oh, cute." It feels very endearing, and I'm being seen when it's used. So the fact that they were making a concerted effort to use it, I was like, that's cool. But, like I said, I'm connected to both.

- How would you apply Whiteness ecology theory to Georgina's story?
- Can you identify representations of the micro, maeso, and macro systems in Georgina's story?
- Based on Whiteness ecology, how does Whiteness play out in Georgina's experiences of name navigation? Can you identify any prevalent themes?
- What have you learnt from Georgina's story?
- How do you aim to implement any learning into your interactions or practice after reading Georgina's story?

11
My name is Musarrat

Developing insights into navigating name identity in Global North and South contexts

- Readers will consider the nuances of name navigation in Global North and South contexts.
- Readers can draw from the Whiteness ecology theory application that the author has modelled in previous chapters to attempt their application to this story.

My name and its cultural ties

So, let's start with my full name. That might help as a good beginning. So, my name is Musarrat Maisha Reza. So, there's like three parts to it. And I go by Maisha, which is my middle name. That surprises many people because people usually use their first name, whose middle name is generally silent, or they have it there because their parents gave it to them. Now, Musarrat Maisha Reza, the three of them, they're all Arabic names. They're their derivatives of words from the Quran. That's what I understand. And Musarrat was a name given to me by my dad's mother. And it's exciting because we are all cultural. I'm Bengali and Muslim, and as family values and family ties are involved, the parents and grandparents also play a massive role in our lives.

So, my dad's mum wanted to name me, and she called me Musarrat; my mother named me Maisha. And so that became my middle name. So it became Musarrat Maisha. And then, obviously, my father's name is Murtaza Reza. And then I picked up his surname, Reza, at the back of my name.

Growing up

Musarrat, because I grew up in Singapore, it's a Chinese majority. So, most of my friends were Chinese, and they had a lot of difficulty pronouncing Musarrat. It used to be Muzrat, Muzarat, and a whole bunch of other permutations and combinations. Sometimes people started making fun of it, and they started seeing mouse rats and many other things. And I mean, they were all nine-, ten-year-old children like myself.

So, everyone's done it with no evil intention per se. But also, teachers couldn't necessarily pronounce it correctly. And so I didn't want to be correcting and attracting too much attention then. And also, we all have favourite grandmas. I love both my grandmothers, but I'm closer to my mum's mum because we always had more things to gossip about. So, Maisha soon became more of my comfort name, my favourite name, and the name that people found easier to pronounce because it's two syllables, right? It's Mai and Sha, so, Maisha. Even then, I have friends ask, "Can I call you Maishi?" I'm like, please. We'll stick to Maisha. We don't have to make a … I'm very protective of that particular name, Maisha, because it connects me to my grandmother. That's my mother's mum, and she's still alive. Alhamdulillah. But I'm like, she's my best friend. My dad's mum passed away. So, Musarrat, it's a lovely memory of her as well. It kind of still connects you to someone who's not living anymore. So, I like that name. I wouldn't say I liked it because it was a complicated name for people to pronounce. I mean, people who didn't share the same ethnicity as me. And it was so difficult for them to pronounce that I found it was difficult or it could be a topic for bullies.

So, I'm just going to keep that name private. At some point, although my full name in the documentation was always Musarrat Maisha Reza, I would eliminate that when talking to people. I'm, oh, I'm Maisha Reza, or if I have to write anything unofficially, I would say Maisha Reza; I would not even talk about my first name.

Temptations to abbreviate or anglicise the name?

Okay, so, in my family, my parents never had a nickname for me or my brother. So we're a small family. I was called my middle name, Maisha, and my brother Maher was called Maher. We never had nicknames like that, probably like darling, my love, like that kind of thing in Bengali, but different from a nickname of our name. So we always had that. So we've always been very proud of it. I couldn't respond to anything else. And so, I didn't know what to abbreviate it to really. I found it very strange when people would abbreviate their names and say them slightly Westernised or English to try to make it comfortable for other people.

I didn't understand that. I know now as to why people do it. And I can see why people do it. But I have a slight advantage because

Musarrat was a more complex name. I had another one to choose from, which was two syllables. So, I have more options if you like. Okay, come to Musarrat. Never mind, we'll go to Musa. And Maisha sounds like a more accessible name. And it is my name, and it is part of my name. Many people call me Reza because those who've never seen me when they start writing your emails call you Reza. And then I used to correct them, and I'd be like, no, I'm Maisha because Reza is my father's name.

But now, somehow, Alhamdulillah, my father's alive as well, but it's just that when they call me Reza, or they start with Dr Reza, I kind of like it because I love my dad, and he's an integral part of me and I'm everything I am is because of my parents, right? So, when people call me Reza, I no longer correct it. They figure it out over time. But I like it. I like it because it almost feels like they're identifying me now in a professional space as Reza. My dad's hard work to give me everything I needed to be where I am today is just coming through. So, I'm a bit too emotional, but …

The turning point

But since I've gotten my PhD, that's when you have to put your full name for publications and stuff. And that's when I slowly started. I don't know what the turning point would be, per se. Maybe it's after my grandmother died; I just started using the entirety of my name. So, everywhere I am, I'm like, hi, I'm Musarrat Maisha Reza, you can call me Maisha.

My email signatures, academic profiles, LinkedIn page, everything has the full name in there because it is part of my identity. Whether or not I liked the sound of it as a child, it is part of my identity, and

I should be more proud of myself as I grow into adulthood and care a little less about what people think. So, I started taking a lot of pride in my full name, but the middle part is still my favourite.

- How would you apply Whiteness ecology theory to Musarrat's story?
- Can you identify representations of the micro, maeso, and macro systems in Musarrat's story?
- Based on Whiteness ecology, how does Whiteness play out in Musarrat's experiences of name navigation? Can you identify any prevalent themes?
- What have you learnt from Musarrat's story?
- How do you aim to implement any learning into your interactions or practice after reading Musarrat's story?

12
My name is Suryani

To develop insights into factors that can steer a person to shorten or change their name

- Readers will better understand factors that can influence name changes or the adoption of different name identities.
- Gain insight into the identity and decision factors that can impact individuals towards their identity formation.
- Readers can draw from the Whiteness ecology theory application that the author has modelled in previous chapters to attempt their application to this story.

My name and the meaning behind it

Okay. I will go for my full name because it has a lot of meaning to it. So, my full name is Suryani Eleanor King. It's a combination of both of my heritages. I was Indonesian and also of my British heritage. Suryani and Eleanor are actually both my grandmothers' names. So, my Indonesian maternal grandmother is called Suryani. And then my British grandmother was called Eleanor. So, my parents just decided on both names. Both of them have quite a good significance as well.

But I do go by Yani. And the reason why … There's a long story about it, that one, because my parents call me Yani. I discovered the reason why behind this. One is because it's a shorter version of Suryani. Still, my Indonesian heritage is also Chinese-Indonesian, and because of the genocide there and the persecution of Chinese people in Indonesia, they had to hide themselves. I had to assimilate to have Indonesian names. So, Suryani is derived from the Chinese name of Soyan. So, Yan is Yani. Also, my parents sometimes call me Yan because of that. So, those two things mixed.

So, Suryani is a very traditional Indonesian name. Whenever I try to tell someone what Suryani is like in Indonesia, it's like the equivalent of Margaret or an ancient name. It means the wife of the sun or the sun goddess. It was initially from the Sanskrit. Eleanor, I discovered a few years ago that it means sun star. So, I feel a lot of connection to my name with being sunny, warm, and bright. It has taken on to my personality. A lot of people who knew my grandmother in Indonesia, unfortunately, I never got to meet her, always say, "You're very similar" to my grandmother. So, I feel like I've embodied it, and I love that. I love my name because it takes my whole family and heritage, and I love that part of my identity.

Growing up and my journey to "Yani"

I prefer to go by Yani because people couldn't get my name right when I moved to the UK. So, when I was about six, I moved to the UK, and I still went by Suryani by everyone, but no one could say my name. So, it bothered me. So, everyone used to call me Sirani, Siryani. And then, I used to get reduced to a dish because when you say Siryani, it sounded like Biryani. So, they called me Biryani or Biri, and I wouldn't say I liked that.

And then, sometimes, some other kids would also call me Sausage Sunny and then Sunny. And I was just like, that wasn't my name. It wasn't who I was. And then, when I went to secondary school, it was a moment of, like, I can correct this, and also, my parents hated hearing my friends call me these names. So, when I got to secondary school, it was like a reset button. Let's go for Yani, and everyone can say that. But living in the South, people have an "ah" sound. So, it was like Yah-ni, and that drives me mad. So, I used to have to be like correcting people, saying Yani. But then, that also got reduced down to Ani. So, I was constantly correcting people, saying Yani, Ani. But when I go up North, everyone has an "a" sound. Everyone can say my name, and it's much more manageable.

Before I talked about my dad being extreme. He is the White British side. He is very proud of my difference. Even if in the middle of this white town in the south of England, he'd always be like, "Okay, we are going to go and explore this thing because it's part of your heritage", and he was the one who was like, "Why are people calling you this? You shouldn't be called Yani. This is what your name is." He was very like, I don't know. That's where I got the strength. It's the same with my mom. She was always like, "This is Yani." So, it's that strength from my parents who said, "No, I don't want you to be called like this. This is your name." So, yeah.

Before I shortened it, it was a solid connection with my family, which I wanted to keep. It was very personal because no one spoke to me as Suryani unless you're my more prominent family. My parents always called me Yani or Yan. When the parents say Suryani, it is like, "Oh, they're going to tell me off." So, that's why I wanted to keep it. When I learned about the whole Chinese heritage and how it influences names, I felt more connected and comfortable being Yani. One thing I own as Suryani: even when connecting through LinkedIn, I still keep my name as Suryani.

If I went on a job application, I would want people to see my name and be very proud of it. I know many people say that there have been studies that if you have a non-anglicised name … No, I want people to see that because I'm very proud of my heritage, and I want people to accept me for who I am and accept my Indonesian heritage. It's a massive part of me. It's part of every-where of me. I want people to show that. Even if I go to Yani, it's still like they'll first know me as "this is me, who I am". This is Suryani, and I get to control that whole thing. Thinking of reflection, I never really had that control when I was a kid. But now, as an adult, I have control over my name. That's an exciting way to think about that. I never thought of that that way.

Professionally, I still go as Yani. But it's only the first time you've met me. You'll hear me as Suryani because it's a mark of, like, this is who I am. I don't know why; I feel it's a vital identity, like my heritage is in my name. It's so strongly, like, you see, Suryani, "Okay, you can tell it's a mixed name." So, I want people to understand that. And then, from Yani, it's when you get closer. Does that make sense?

I have even considered it more recently but considered changing everything, even turning to just Yani. But then, I decided no because I was like, losing your identity in that bit, and I'm like, "No, I don't want to lose that ever." And then, I had the thing of brackets, Yani, and I was like, "This is perfect." I get to have both.

I'm very comfortable. I still really love my name. I love every meaning behind it and that my parents gave it to me. When I was a kid, I was so self-conscious of my name and being in a white town and being one of the only mixed heritage kids or even being like any of the white. I wanted to change my name. This sounds so … I mean, I think it's dumb, but also, it's kid logic, which I think is funny.

Now, I'm like, "No, I'm Suryani. I go by Yani and am very proud of who I am."

I just became Yani. So, I now have it in my signature at work, saying, "It's like Ani with a Y." But I never really connected that until someone I was talking to, I was like, "Oh, sometimes people get my name wrong, and I don't know what to say. Is there an easy way to explain it?" And they were like, "Well, your name's Ani with a Y", and I was like, "Oh, yeah. I guess that is." So, going back to Ani from what people used to call me, correcting it and being Yani. That's the story of my name.

Getting a name right

Also, with context about moving to the UK, I lived in the South, a predominantly white town. So, when people couldn't say my name, it [had an impact]. It's like the saying "to say my name". It's my name, so just respect that.

- How would you apply Whiteness ecology theory to Suryani's story?
- Can you identify representations of the micro, maeso, and macro systems in Suryani's story?
- Based on Whiteness ecology, how does Whiteness play out in Suryani's experiences of name navigation? Can you identify any prevalent themes?
- What have you learnt from Suryani's story?
- How do you aim to implement any learning into your interactions or practice after reading Suryani's story?

13
The themes

To consolidate learning from all the stories shared in this book

- Readers will consider key themes from across the stories to develop a broader understanding of the issues surrounding name identity.

The stories shared in this book demonstrate that people with "foreign-sounding names" face similar challenges in Western colonial contexts, despite different circumstances. The common themes that emerge across all the stories are the feeling of being marginalised due to the way their name was handled, the negative impact of marginalisation on the individual's identity formation, the racial connotations associated with the navigation of racially marginalised individuals' names, the pressure to anglicise or shorten names for the comfort of others, pressure to assimilate, and fatigue in correcting others' pronunciation of names. Individuals attach significant value to their names, and the correct pronunciation of names has a positive impact on self-confidence.

The stories in this book demonstrate the practical application of Whiteness ecology theory. It explains how racial politics and socio-historical colonial contexts can affect the pronunciation of names belonging to individuals who are part of minoritised racial groups and have foreign-sounding names. The book encourages us to think carefully about the impact of our everyday inter-actions and how even small gestures, such as pronouncing a name correctly, can play a significant role in helping someone assert their identity in the face of complex colonial and racialised politics.

Notes

Chapter 1: Understanding name identity using Whiteness ecology theory

1. Black British in this context references the Jamaican diaspora while acknowledging the broader ramifications emerging from these communities' experiences to inform a "Black British" identity and experience.

Chapter 3: My name is Dheeraj

1. Making a joke at the negative expense of someone.

Recommended discussion topics

Do you think attitudes have changed for the better regarding name bias? Why/Why not?

Following on from the previous question, what does change, or lack of change, represent in the context of a Whiteness ecology?

What do you think Armen's experience speaks to in relation to broader social issues surrounding Whiteness? For instance, how are the maeso and macro systems represented in Armen's story?

Have you experienced or observed name bias? What would you conclude of that direct or observational experience if you were to unpack it using a Whiteness ecology?

Why do you think people are prompted to shorten their names? How does this speak to pressures to "assimilate" to Western norms?

Reflecting on the previous question, what do you think this speaks to in relation to broader societal norms? Connect this to Whiteness ecology, emphasising the different systemic layers that constitute the ecology.

Why would it be difficult for someone to revert to their given name after adopting a different name for so long?

Why are names important? And what do names signify? Think about these two questions in the context of inclusion and belonging. How would an inclusively sound environment approach name? For example, are there opportunities in the spaces you hold for people to correct the pronunciation of their names? If so, how? If not, how can this be implemented?

How can having names changed or experiencing names as a barrier impact one's personal identity? Also consider this question in the context of individuals from the global majority backgrounds. What additional barriers will these individuals encounter in name navigation in a Whiteness ecology?

The film *My Name Is* can be watched for free at www.mynameis documentary.com. The following questions are useful for framing a post-screening discussion.

What have you taken away from the screening today?

How might you implement some of the messages from the film in your own practice and interactions?

References

Bronfenbrenner, U. (1975). Reality and Research in the Ecology of Human Development. *Proceedings of the American Philosophical Society*, 119(6), pp. 439–469. Available at: www.jstor.org/stable/986378.

Etchells, M. J. *et al.* (2017). White Male Privilege: An Intersectional Deconstruction. *Journal of Ethnic and Cultural Studies*, 4(2), pp. 13–27.

Garner, S. (2017). Surfing the Third Wave of Whiteness Studies: Reflections on Twine and Gallagher. *Ethnic and Racial Studies*, 40(9), pp. 1582–1597. doi: 10.1080/01419870.2017.1300301.

Hall, S. (1997). Representation: Cultural representations and signifying practices. In: S. Hall, ed., *Representation: Cultural Representation & Signifying Practices*. SAGE Publications in association with the Open University, pp. 15–39. doi: 10.1177/0898010110393351.

Hong, J.S. and Garbarino, J. (2012). Risk and Protective Factors for Homophobic Bullying in Schools: An Application of the Social–Ecological Framework. Educational Psychology Review, 24(2), pp.271–285. doi:https://doi.org/10.1007/s10648-012-9194-y.

My Name Is. (2022). My Name Is. | Chapter 1: Our Past. [online] YouTube. Available at: www.youtube.com/watch?v=Gq6F3uMA KKY&list=PL6cpEEfXB-xY2V8vwZSRqTmJrhhJsZycJ [Accessed 30 June 2024].

My Name Is. (n.d.). Film Documentary [online]. Available at: https://mynameisdocumentary.com [Accessed 1 July 2024].

Nayak, A. (2007). Critical Whiteness Studies. *Sociology Compass*, 1(2), pp. 737–755. doi: 10.1111/j.1751-9020.2007.00045.x.

Shah, J. K. (2021). An ecological exploration of Whiteness: Using imperial hegemony and racial socialisation to examine lived experiences and social performativity of melanated communities. In: S. Hunter and C. van der Westhuizen, eds., *Routledge Handbook of Critical Studies in Whiteness*. 1st ed. London: Routledge, pp. 313–325. Available at: www.routledge.com/Routledge-Handbook-of-Critical-Studies-in-Whiteness/Hunter-Westhuizen/p/book/9780367403799.

Steer, R. *et al.* (2007). "Modernisation" and the Role of Policy Levers in the Learning and Skills Sector. *Journal of Vocational Education & Training*, 59(2), pp. 175–192. doi: 10.1080/13636820701342574.

Subnormal. (2021). UK: BBC, L. Shannon. Available at: www.bbc.co.uk/programmes/m000w81h.

Recommended further reading

Shah, J. K. (2021). An ecological exploration of Whiteness: Using imperial hegemony and racial socialisation to examine lived experiences and social performativity of melanated communities. In: S. Hunter and C. van der Westhuizen, eds., *Routledge Handbook of Critical Studies in Whiteness*. 1st ed. London: Routledge, pp. 313–325.

Index

www.ingramcontent.com/pod-product-compliance
Lightning Source LLC
Chambersburg PA
CBHW070347270326

41926CB00017B/4033